double knits

double knits

Zoë Mellor

Trafalgar Square Publishing

For my son, Toby Tiger, who is a great joy and inspiration to me.

First published in the United States of America in 2000 by
Trafalgar Square Publishing, North Pomfret, Vermont 05053

Printed in Singapore by Imago

Copyright © Collins & Brown Limited 2000
Text copyright © Zoë Mellor 2000
Illustrations copyright © Collins & Brown Limited 2000
Photographs copyright © Collins & Brown Limited 2000

Library of Congress Catalog Number:
00-101979

ISBN 1-57076-167-1

3 5 7 9 8 6 4 2

EDITOR: Ulla Weinberg
DESIGNER: Luise Roberts
PHOTOGRAPHY: Daniel Pangbourne
STYLING: Zoë Mellor
COPY-EDITOR: Margot Richardson
PATTERN CHECKERS: Eva Yates, Gill Everett

ACKNOWLEDGEMENTS
Thank you to all the fabulous knitters who knitted up my designs with such care and attention. Special thanks to Eva and Gill for their expert pattern checking and to Mike for his patience with those floppy disks!

Thank you also to all the beautiful twins who kindly agreed to model my knits and to their parents for all their encouragement on the photo shoots (especially Rosie and Alice).

Thanks also to Daniel for the gorgeous photos and handy camper van/changing room; and to Luise for the lovely layouts.

Last but not least, thanks to all my family and friends, and especially my son Toby.

Zoë Mellor can be contacted at: 26, Belvedere Terrace, Brighton, East Sussex, BN1 3AF, UK.

SUPPLIERS OF ROWAN YARNS

Australia
Rowan at Sunspun
185 Canterbury Road
Canterbury, Victoria 3126
Tel: 03 9830 1609

Canada
Diamond Yarn
9697 St Laurent, Montreal
Quebec H3L 2N1
Tel: 514 388 6188

Diamond Yarn (Toronto)
155 Martin Ross, Unit 3
Toronto, Ontario M3J 2L9
Tel: 416 736 6111

UK
Rowan Yarns
Green Lane Mill, Holmfirth
HD7 1RW, West Yorkshire
Tel: 01484 681881

Mail order: Selfridges
400 Oxford Street
London, W1A 1AB
Tel: 0171 328 3856

USA
Westminster Fibres Inc.
5 Northern Boulevard
Amherst, New Hampshire 03031
Tel: 603 886 5041/5043

contents

introduction

Since the arrival of my son Toby 18 months ago, I have been wanting to design decorative and contemporary knits specifically for babies and toddlers. I often get asked where Toby's sweaters have come from, so here are some of my favourite new designs. These include the fish sweater and cardigan, the daisy knits, the duffle coats, the Inca hats with their cosy ear flaps, and the cheeky flat cat toys.

At workshops, knitters frequently ask how to change a pattern from a sweater design to a cardigan or vice versa, so in this book there are many patterns that can be made to suit your personal preference. The garments have been photographed using twins for models, each wearing a variation on the same design. This shows the range of options available – make a cardigan or a sweater in the same pattern, change the colourway, or knit both for brothers and sisters!

Being a busy mother myself, I know how important it is to have patterns that are quick and easy to knit, and although I love colourful knitting there are quite a few single colour designs for those who prefer textured knitting.

I hope you will have as much fun knitting these – and seeing them worn by the child in your life – as I had designing them. Happy knitting!

Zoë Mellor

daisy sweater and cardigan

This sweater and cardigan are bright and bold in design with a punchy daisy motif. The sweater features a large daisy, whereas the cardigan has plenty of little daisies and a moss-stitch collar. They share a distinctive and pretty pointed edging.

PATTERNS PAGES 49–52

patchwork blankets

These baby blankets are simple to knit and striking to look at. The cotton yarn is soft on babies' delicate skin and easy to wash, and the simple pink heart or blue star motifs are ideal for either boys or girls.

PATTERN PAGE 53

inca hats

Keep little heads extra warm with these cosy hats and their added ear flaps. They look wonderful in either the pink or the green colourway, and will become treasured favourites.

PATTERNS PAGES 54–5

13

heart and star patch sweaters

These sweaters in powder pinks and soft blues are a bolder way to wear pastels. They have contrasting textured patches for added interest, and buttoned shoulder openings for easy wear.

PATTERNS PAGES 56–7

14

breton cardigan and sweater

Perfect for a trip to the seaside, here are a sweater and cardigan in a classic French look with modern moss-stitch edgings. The cardigan has a double-breasted buttonband and the sweater has a buttoned shoulder opening for easy dressing and undressing. Sew the buttons on with red thread for dramatic detail.

PATTERNS PAGES 58–9

baby sundress and all-in-one

This lovely classic duet of
sundress and all-in-one is
made from soft cotton and
is therefore great for sunny
days. They both have
buttoned straps, making
them easy to get on and off.

nursery sweaters

Teach your little ones their 123s and ABCs with these colourful picture knits. Both styles have buttons on the shoulder for easy dressing; the pale blue version comes with a pretty pointed edging while the navy sweater has a straight hem.

PATTERNS PAGES 62–3

moss-stitch cardigan and tunic

PATTERNS PAGES 64–5

A great pair of modern knits, showing off the beautiful texture of moss stitch. The tunic, with its Robin Hood-style collar, and the classic cardigan are both stylish and easy to make – suitable for any busy mother to knit.

candy-striped sweater and cardigan

Here are two bold, stripy knits that are great fun and simple to make. The sweater has a lime green edge on the neckband, cuffs and hem, while the cardigan has a moss-stitch collar and edgings in dark blue that show off the bright colours to perfection.

PATTERNS PAGES 66–7

little people cardigan and sweater

Perfect for little people who are snappy dressers, both cardigan and sweater have a pretty pointed edging in moss stitch. The sweater is finished with a contrasting red edging, and the smaller sizes have a buttoned shoulder opening.

PATTERNS PAGES 68–71

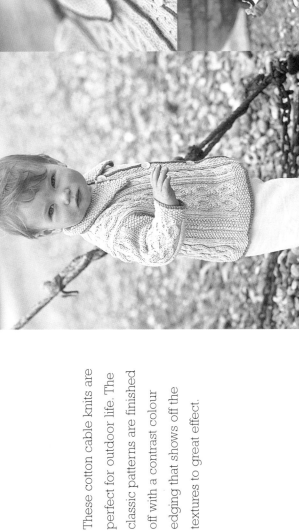

These cotton cable knits are perfect for outdoor life. The classic patterns are finished off with a contrast colour edging that shows off the textures to great effect.

aran sweater and cardigan

PATTERNS PAGES 72–5

29

bear and tiger hats

Great for cold winter walks, these cuddly hats, with their delightful knitted ears, are bound to make you smile.

PATTERNS PAGE 76

duffle coats

Lovely, simple, double-breasted jackets that are quick to knit and long enough to keep out the cold. They look great in orange or blue chunky tweed yarn.

PATTERNS PAGES 77–8

33

jester booties

These cheerful booties can be knitted in a multitude of colourways, using different-coloured bobbles and contrasting soles, tops and edging. Ankle cuffs keep the booties snugly on baby's feet.

PATTERN PAGE 79

34

stripy bag

Stripy bags are loved by adults and children alike. These can be knitted either in stylish pastel or vibrant candy stripes, and are complemented with a random, pointed edging for a pretty finish.

PATTERN PAGE 80

mexican cardigan and sweater

The colourful cardigan, with fun bird and flower motifs, has a cerise collar, cuffs and buttonband. The sweater variation has a buttoned shoulder opening. Both feature pointed edging around the waist.

PATTERNS PAGES 81–3

38

fairisle jacket and sweater

These traditional fairisle knits, with their scalloped lacy edgings on the hem, are perfect for little girls. The cardigan has a practical moss-stitch collar and is finished with classic mother-of-pearl buttons.

PATTERNS PAGES 84–6

41

lacy sweater and cardigan

These delicate and pretty knits have a clever scalloped edging that leads into the lacy panels. The sweater has a moss-stitch neckband and cuffs, and buttons on the shoulder for easy dressing; the cardigan is finished with a moss-stitch collar and looks great both for everyday wear and for special occasions.

PATTERNS PAGES 87–90

42

fish sweater and cardigan

This eye-catching smiling fish sweater is great fun and will be loved by all little fishermen. The sweater is slightly more bold, with its colourful single-fish panel, while the cardigan's all-over fish design can be complemented by other colourful clothing. Both designs share a bobbing-boat border and modern rolled edgings in a contrasting colour.

PATTERNS PAGES 91–4

45

flat cats

These cheeky cats can be knitted in lots of different colourways. A great way to use up spare yarn, they are easy enough for even the youngest of knitters to attempt, and are bound to become family favourites.

pattern index

daisy sweater

TENSION

20 sts by 28 rows = 10cm (4in) square over stocking stitch using 4mm (US 6) needles.

ABBREVIATIONS

See page 96.

BACK

Using 4mm (US 6) needles and M, cast on 61(67:75) sts and work in stocking stitch as follows:

ROWS 1–4: as border graph. Work further 2(6:10) rows in M.

ROW 7(11:15): place daisy, k30(33:37)M, 1 ecru, k30(33:37)M.

Cont to completion of daisy. *(Row 64:68:72)*.

Cont to completion of row 75(81:91).

Shape neck:

Sizes 1 and 2: NEXT ROW: (WS facing) patt 22 sts, turn.

ROWS 2–3: dec neck edge.

ROWS 4–6: change to 3¼mm (US 3) needles and using M, work in k2 p2 rib.

ROW 7: cast off in rib.

Place centre 17(23) sts on holder. Rejoin yarns to remaining sts at neck edge, patt to end. Dec neck edge on next 2 rows. Cast off.

Size 3: NEXT ROW: (WS facing), patt 25 sts, turn. *Dec neck edge on next two rows. Cast off*. Place centre 25 sts on holder.

Rejoin yarn to remaining sts at neck edge, patt to end. Work * to * again.

FRONT

As back to completion of row 65(71:79).

Shape neck:

NEXT ROW: (WS facing), p26(28:31) sts, turn. Dec neck edge on next 6(8:7) rows.

Continue to completion of row 78(84:94). Cast off. Place centre 9(11:13) sts on holder. Rejoin yarns to remaining sts at neck, purl to end. Dec neck edge on next 6(8:7) rows. Work to completion of row 73(79:94).

Size 3: cast off.

Sizes 1 and 2: NEXT ROW: using M, p4 p2tog yrn p7 p2tog yrn p5.

p2tog yrn p7 p2tog yrn p5. Change to 3¼mm (US 3) needles, work 3 rows in k2 p2 rib. Change to yellow and purl 1 row. Cast off in yellow.

SLEEVES

Using 3¼mm (US 3) needles and M, cast on 33(35:37) sts.

ROWS 1–6: moss stitch.

Change to 4mm (US 6) needles and stocking stitch, inc each end of 5th and every foll 4th row working in patt as follows:

ROWS 1–4: border graph. Work further 4(8:12) rows in M.

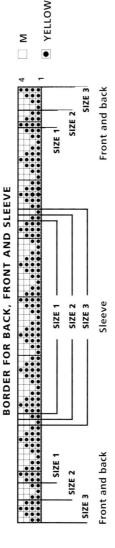

SIZES

	1	2	3
to fit years	6mths–1	1–2	2–3
actual chest cm(in)	59(23)	66(26)	74(29)
back length	29(11½)	32(12½)	36(14)
sleeve seam	18(7)	20(8)	25(10)

YARN

Rowan DK cotton 50g balls

	1	2	3
☐ red (M)	5	6	7
● yellow	1	1	1
╱ ecru	1	1	1

BUTTONS

3 small buttons (size 1 & 2).

NEEDLES

1 pair each of 3¼mm (US 3) and 4mm (US 6) needles. Stitch holders.

☐ M

● YELLOW

BORDER FOR BACK, FRONT AND SLEEVE

SIZE 1
SIZE 2
SIZE 3

Front and back

Sleeve

SIZE 1
SIZE 2
SIZE 3

4
1
SIZE 1
SIZE 2
SIZE 3

Front and back

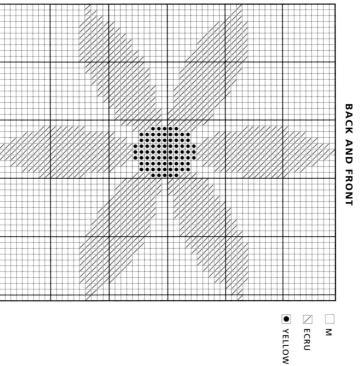

BACK AND FRONT

□ M
▨ ECRU
● YELLOW

ROW 7(11,15)

SLEEVE

ROW 9(13,17)

daisy sweater

ROWS 9(13:17): place daisy, inc, k16(18:20)M,
1 ecru, k16(18:20), inc.
Cont to completion of daisy motif, inc every
4th row to 53(57:63) sts. Cont without
shaping until work measures 18(20:25)cm
(7:8:10in). Cast off.

NECKBAND
Join left shoulder seam. With RS facing and
using 3¼mm (US 3) needles and M, pick up
and knit 38(40:44) sts from front neck and
28(32:32) sts from back neck.
Sizes 1 and 2: work 2 rows k2 p2 rib.
ROW 3: rib 62(68), dec, yrn, rib 2.
ROW 4: rib.
ROW 5: change to yellow, purl.
ROW 6: cast off loosely in yellow.
Size 3: work 4 rows in k2 p2 rib.
ROWS 5–6: as sizes 1 and 2.

POINTED EDGING
Using 4mm (US 6) needles and M, cast on 2 sts.
ROW 1: k2.
ROW 2: inc, k1.
ROW 3: k1 p1 inc.
ROW 4: inc, k1 p1 k1.
ROWS 5–8: moss stitch, inc at shaped edge on
every row. **(9 sts)**
ROW 9: moss stitch.
ROWS 10–15: dec at shaped edge on each
row, moss stitch. **(2 sts)**
Repeat rows 1–16 until straight edge fits
lower edge of garment, ending after a
complete patt repeat.

MAKING UP
Sizes 1 and 2: pin right shoulder overlap
into place. ✱ Measure 12(13:14)cm
(4¾:5:5½in) down from shoulder seam, place
pin. Set in sleeves between pins and stitch.
Join sleeve and side seam. Weave in any
loose ends. Sew on buttons. Sew pointed
edging to hem. ✱
Size 3: join right shoulder seam and
neckband. Work ✱ to ✱ as for sizes 1 and 2:
no buttons.

50

daisy cardigan

SIZES

SIZES	1	2	3
to fit years	6mths–1	1–2	2–3
actual chest cm(in)	61(24)	66(26)	71(28)
back length	29(11½)	32(12½)	36(14)
sleeve seam	18(7)	20(8)	25(10)

YARN

Rowan DK cotton 50g balls

	1	2	3
☐ blue (M)	4	5	6
⊞ ecru	1	1	2
☒ yellow	1	1	1

BUTTONS

5 buttons.

NEEDLES

1 pair each of 3¼mm (US 3) and 4mm (US 6) needles.

TENSION

20 sts by 28 rows = 10cm (4in) square over stocking stitch using 4mm (US 6) needles.

ABBREVIATIONS

See page 96.

BACK

Using 4mm (US 6) needles and M, cast on 61(65:71) sts. Working in stocking stitch, follow graph. Start size 2 on row 11.

RIGHT AND LEFT FRONTS

Using 4mm (US 6) needles and M cast on 30(32:35) sts. Working in stocking stitch, follow graph. Start size 2 on row 11.

SLEEVES

Using 3¼mm (US 3) needles and M cast on 33(35:37) sts and work 8(6:10) rows in moss stitch. (Every row = *k1 p1* to last st, k1). Change to 4mm (US 6) needles and stocking stitch, follow graph.

POINTED EDGING

Work as for sweater (see page 50).

BUTTONBAND

Using 3¼mm (US 3) needles and M, cast on 6 sts and work in moss stitch until band, when slightly stretched, fits front to neck shaping. Cast off. Sew into place. Mark positions for 5 buttons, the first and last 1cm (½in) from top and bottom edges and the remaining 3 evenly spaced between.

BUTTONHOLE BAND

Work to match buttonband, making buttonholes to match button positions by: moss 2, k2tog, yrn, moss 2.

COLLAR

Join shoulder seams. Using 3¼mm (US 3) needles and M with right side facing and beginning and ending at centre of front bands, pick up and knit 67(73:77) sts from neck. Work as follows:

ROWS 1–2: k2, moss to last 2 sts, k2
ROW 3: k2, moss to last 3 sts, inc, k2
Repeat row 3 until collar measures 6cm (2½in). Cast off loosely in moss stitch.

MAKING UP

Measure 12(13:14)cm (4¾:5:5½in) down from shoulder seam, place pin. Set in sleeves between pins and stitch. Join sleeve and side seams. Weave in any loose ends. Sew on pointed edging to hem, omitting front bands. Sew on buttons.

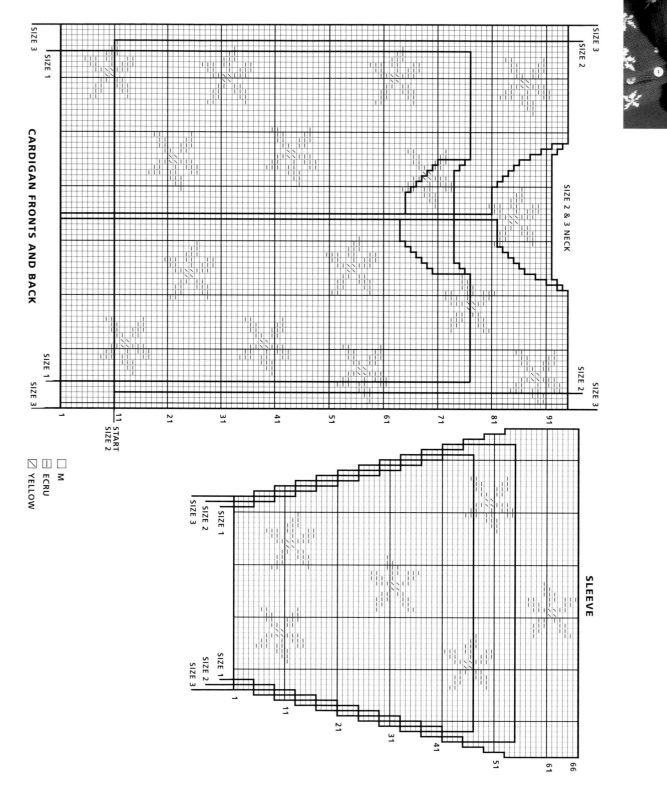

CARDIGAN FRONTS AND BACK

SIZE 3
SIZE 2
SIZE 1

SIZE 2 & 3 NECK

SIZE 1
SIZE 3
SIZE 2
SIZE 3

1 11 21 31 41 51 61 71 81 91
START
SIZE 2

☐ M
⊡ ECRU
◪ YELLOW

52

SLEEVE

SIZE 2
SIZE 1
SIZE 3

SIZE 1
SIZE 2
SIZE 3

1 11 21 31 41 51 61 66

patchwork blankets

TENSION
20 sts by 28 rows = 10cm (4in) square over stocking stitch using 4mm (US 6) needles.

ABBREVIATIONS
See page 96.

MOSS-STITCH PATCHES
Cast on 25 sts. Work 37 rows in moss stitch, [every row: *k1 p1* to last st, k1].
Cast off in moss stitch.
Make 7 using B, 5 using A and 5 using C.

HEART OR STAR PATCHES
Using background colour, cast on 25 sts and working in stocking stitch and using intarsia technique, follow graph. Cast off.

Number	Background	Contrast
4	B	A
2	B	C
3	A	B
3	A	C
3	C	B
3	C	A

MAKING UP
Lay out squares on a flat surface, making 7 rows of 5 squares, alternating motif and moss-stitch squares.

ROW 1: (motif, moss) 2, motif;
ROW 2: (moss, motif) 2, moss;
ROWS 3–6: as rows 1–2 twice;
ROW 7: as row 1], ensuring that the same colours are not side by side. Number the squares so you remember the sequence. Stitch them together, using a flat seam to avoid any bulk at the back of the work.

EDGINGS
Using 4mm (US 6) needles and A, cast on 2 sts, work as follows, starting with mitre corner.

ROW 1: k2.
ROW 2: inc, k1.
ROW 3: k1 p1, inc.
ROW 4: inc, k1 p1 k1.
ROWS 5–10: moss stitch, inc at shaped edge on every row. *(11 sts)*
Cont in moss stitch until shorter edge, when slightly stretched, fits side of blanket. Work 10 more rows, dec 1 st per row, making sure that you start dec at the shorter edge, to make mitre corner.
Make three more pieces to fit the other side, top and bottom of blanket.
Attach the edging to all four sides, and join the mitred corners. Weave in any loose ends.

SIZE
Width 70cm(27½in)
Length 96cm(38in)

YARN
Rowan DK cotton 50g balls

	Colourway 1 (Hearts)	Colourway 2 (Stars)	No.
A	light pink	dark blue	5
B	ecru	ecru	4
C	dark pink	light blue	4

NEEDLES
1 pair 4mm (US 6) needles.

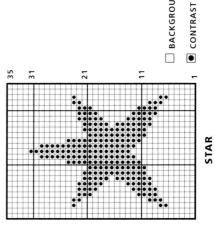

☐ BACKGROUND
⦿ CONTRAST

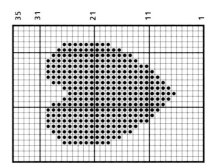

STAR

HEART

53

inca hats

TENSION
23 sts by 30 rows = 10cm (4in) square over stocking stitch using 4mm (US 6) needles.

ABBREVIATIONS
See page 96.

EAR FLAPS (2)
Using 4mm (US 6) needles and M, cast on 7(9:11) sts and work in stocking stitch as follows:

ROW 1: inc each end.
ROW 2: inc * 1A 1M * to last st, inc.
ROW 3: *1A 1M* to last st, 1A.
ROW 4: A, inc each end.
ROW 5: inc B, *1A 1B* to last 2 sts, 1A, inc B.
ROW 6: * 1A 1B * to last st, 1A.
ROW 7: B, inc each end. (17:19:21 sts)
ROW 8: B.
ROW 9: * 1B 1M* to last st, 1B.
ROW 10: M.
ROWS 11-12: * 1A 1M * to last st, 1A.
ROW 13: A.
ROWS 14-15: * 1A 1B* to last st, 1A.
Size 1: leave sts on spare needle.
Size 2: ROW 16: B.
ROW 17: M, leave sts on spare needle.
Size 3: ROW 16: B.
ROW 17: M, leave sts on spare needle.
ROWS 17-18: *1M 1B* to last st, 1M.
ROW 19: M, leave sts on spare needle.

MAIN HAT
Using 3¾mm (US 5) needles and M, cast on 12(14:17) sts, purl across ear flap, cast on 32(36:44) sts, purl across ear flap, cast on 12(14:17) sts. (90:102:120 sts)

Work as follows:

ROW 1: RS facing, using M, purl.
ROWS 2-3: using C, purl.
ROW 4: using M, purl.
Change to 4mm (US 6) needles and stocking stitch. Work rows 1-16 from graph.
ROWS 17-18: using B, knit.

Size 2:
ROW 19: knit * 2M 2A* to last 2 sts, 2M.
ROW 20: purl 2togM * 2A 2M * to last 4 sts, 2A 2togM. (100 sts)

Size 3:
ROW 19: knit * 2M 2A* to end.
ROW 20: purl * 2A 2M* to end.
ROW 21: knit * 2A 2M * to end.
ROW 22: purl * 2M 2A* to end.

Shape top: (all sizes) work in stocking stitch.
ROW 1: M.
ROW 2: *p2tog, p8* to end.
ROW 3: * 1M 1B* to last 1(0:0) sts, 1(0:0)M.
ROW 4: 1(0:0)M * 1B 1M* to end.
ROW 5: using B, *k7 k2tog* to end.
ROW 6: C.
ROW 7: * 1A 1M* to end.
ROW 8: [p2togM *1M 1A* 3 times] to end.
ROW 9: A.
ROW 10: B.
ROW 11: [2B 1C 2B k2togC] to end. (54:60:72 sts)

FAIRISLE PATTERN

Key:
☐ M
⊡ A
◇ C
⊟ B

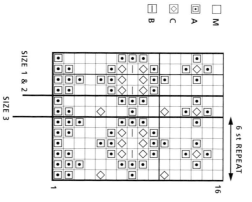

SIZE 1 & 2
SIZE 3
PURL ROWS START
6 st REPEAT
1 — 16

inca hats

Size 1:
ROW 12: using B, * p2tog p4 * to end.
ROW 13: * 1M 1B 1M k2togB * to end.
ROW 14: * p2togM * to end.
ROW 15: * k2togM * to end.

Size 2:
ROW 12: B.
ROW 13: [* 1M 1B * twice, k2togM] to end.
ROW 14: 1M * 1B 1M 2M * to last 4 sts,
*1B 1M * twice.
ROW 15: using M, * k3 k2tog * to end. (*40 sts*)
ROW 16: using C, * p2tog * to end
ROW 17: using A, * k2tog * to end.

Size 3:
ROWS 12–15: as Size 2.
ROW 16: *1M 2A 1M * to end.
ROW 17: using A, * k2 k2tog * to end.
ROW 18: using C, * p2tog p1 * to end.
ROW 19: using M, * k2tog *.

All sizes: thread yarn through remaining
sts, draw tightly and fasten off securely.

EDGING
With RS facing and using 3¾mm (US 5)
needles and M, pick up and knit
12(14:17) sts from back cast-on edge,
31(37:43) sts around ear flap, 32(36:44) sts
from front cast-on edge, 31(37:43) sts
around ear flap and 12(14:17) sts from back
cast-on edge. Cast off knitwise.

MAKING UP
Join back seam. Weave in any loose ends.
Cut three 60cm (24in) lengths of M. Thread
half the length through bottom centre of ear
flap. Taking one end from front and one end
from back, make a plait with two ends per
strand. Knot at end and trim. Repeat for
second ear flap.

SIZES

SIZES	1	2	3
to fit years	6mths–1	1–2	2–3

YARN
Rowan Designer DK wool 50g balls

		Colourway 1	Colourway 2	No.
☐	M	dark pink	green	1
⊡	A	pale pink	blue	1
⊟	B	ecru	ecru	1
◇	C	yellow	yellow	1

NEEDLES
1 pair each of 3¾mm (US 5) and 4mm (US 6) needles.
Spare needle.

heart and star patch sweaters

TENSION
24 sts by 32 rows = 10cm (4in) square over stocking stitch using 3¼mm (US 3) needles.

ABBREVIATIONS
See page 96.

BACK
Using 2¾mm (US 2) needles and A, cast on 73(79:85) sts and work 10 rows in moss stitch. Change to 3¼mm (US 3) needles and work as follows:

NB: Use intarsia method.

ROW 1: knit 0(2:5)B, 14(15:15)C, 15B, 15A, 14(15:15)A, 0(2:5)B.

ROW 2: moss 0(2:5)B, p14(15:15)A, 15B, p15A, moss 0(2:5)B.

ROW 3: moss 0(2:5)B, k14(15:15)C, moss 15B, k15A, moss 15B, k14(15:15)A, moss 0(2:5)B.

ROW 4: HEART: moss 0(2:5)B, p6(7:7)A 1C 7A, moss 15B, p7A 1B 7A, moss 15B, p7C 1A 6(7:7)C, moss 0(2:5)B.
STAR: moss 0(2:5)B, p1(2:2)A 1C 9A 1C 2A, moss 15B, p2A 1B 9A 1B 2A, moss 15B, p2C 1A 9C 1A (2:2)C, moss 0(2:5)B.

ROWS 5–20: cont moss patches as set and motif patches from graph.

ROW 21: knit 0(2:5)A, 14(15:15)B, 15A, 15C, 14(15:15)C, 0(2:5)A.

ROW 22: p0(2:5)A, moss 14(15:15)C, p15A, moss 15C, p15A, moss 14(15:15)B, p0(2:5)A.

ROW 23: k0(2:5)A, moss 14(15:15)B, k15A, moss 15C, k15A, moss 14(15:15)C, k0(2:5)A.

ROW 24: HEART: p0(2:5)A, moss 14(15:15)C, k7A 1B 7A, moss 15C, k7A 1C 7A, moss 14(15:15)B, k0(2:5)A.
STAR: p0(2:5)A, moss14(15:15)C, k2A 1B 9A 1B 2A, moss 15C, k2A 1C 9A 1C 2A, moss 14(15:15)B, p0(2:5)A.

ROWS 25–40: as rows 5–20.

These 40 rows set patch repeats.

COLOURS FOR ROWS 41–60: patches, C, A, C, B, C, B, C; motifs, C, A, B.

COLOURS FOR ROWS 61–80: patches as rows 1–20, motifs C, A.

COLOURS FOR ROWS 81–100: patches as rows 21–40, motifs A, B, C.

COLOURS FOR ROWS 101–120: patches as rows 41–60, motifs A, B.

Cont until work measures 29(32:36)cm (11½:12½:14in) ending with RS row.

☐ BACKGROUND
● CONTRAST

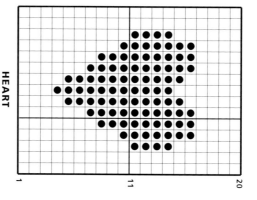

HEART

1
11
20

Shape neck: NEXT ROW: (WS facing) patt 25(27:29) sts, turn.

ROWS 2–3: dec neck edge.

ROW 4: change to 2¾mm (US 2) needles and using A, knit.

ROWS 5–6: moss stitch.

ROW 7: cast off in moss stitch.
Place centre 23(25:27) sts on holder. Rejoin yarns to remaining sts at neck edge, patt to end. Dec neck edge on next 2 rows. Cast off.

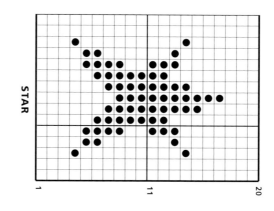

STAR

1
11
20

SIZES	1	2	3
to fit years	6mths–1	1–2	2–3
actual chest cm(in)	61(24)	66(26)	71(28)
back length	29(11½)	32(12½)	36(14)
sleeve seam	18(7)	20(8)	25(10)

YARN

Rowan Cotton Glacé 50g balls

Hearts

A	dark pink	3	3	4
B	light pink	2	2	2
C	ecru	2	2	2

Stars

A	dark blue	3	3	4
B	light blue	2	2	2
C	ecru	2	2	2

BUTTONS

3 small buttons.

NEEDLES

1 pair each of 2¾mm (US 2) and 3¼mm (US 3) needles. Stitch holders.

heart and star patch sweaters

FRONT

As back until work measures 25(27:29)cm (10:10½:11½in).

Shape neck: NEXT ROW: (WS facing), patt 31(33:35) sts, turn. Dec neck edge on next 8 rows (23:25:27 sts), cont to match back at shoulder. Cast off. Place centre 11(13:15) sts on holder. Rejoin yarns to remaining sts at neck, patt to end. Dec neck edge on next 8 rows. Work to 3 rows less than first side.

NEXT ROW: using M, p5(6:7) p2tog yrn p8 p2tog yrn p6(7:8).

Change to 2¾mm (US 2) needles, work 4 rows in moss stitch. Cast off in moss stitch.

SLEEVES

Using 2¾mm (US 2) needles and A, cast on 35(37:39) sts and work 10 rows in moss stitch.

Change to 3¼mm (US 3) needles and work as follows:

ROWS 1–2: using B, stocking stitch.

ROW 3: using A, knit, inc each end.

ROWS 4–22: using A, moss st, inc each end of rows 7, 11, 15 and 19.

ROWS 23–24: using C, stocking stitch, inc each end of row 23.

ROW 25: using A, knit.

ROWS 26–44: using A, moss stitch, inc each end of rows 27, 31, 35, 39, and 43.

ROWS 1–44: form sleeve patt. Cont as set, inc every 4th row to 57(61:65) sts. Cont without shaping until work measures 18(20:25)cm (7:8:10in). Cast off.

NECKBAND

Join left shoulder seam. With RS facing and using 2¾mm (US 2) needles and M, pick up and knit 14(16:18) sts from side front neck, 11(13:15) sts from holder, 14(16:18) sts from side front neck, 1 st from shoulder seam, 34(36:38) sts from back neck.

ROWS 1–2: moss stitch.

ROW 3: moss to last 3 sts, yrn p2tog k2.

ROW 4–5: moss stitch.

ROW 6: cast off loosely.

MAKING UP

Pin right shoulder overlap into place. Measure 12(13:14)cm (4¾:5:5½in) down from shoulder seam, place pin. Set in sleeves between pins and stitch. Join sleeve and side seam. Weave in any loose ends. Sew on buttons.

breton cardigan and sweater

TENSION

23 sts by 30 rows = 10cm (4in) square over stocking stitch using 4mm (US 6) needles.

ABBREVIATIONS

See page 96.

Cardigan

BACK

Using 3¼mm (US 3) needles and M, cast on 69(75:81) sts and work 10 rows in moss stitch, (every row *k1 p1 * to last st, k1). Change to 4mm (US 6) needles and stocking stitch. Work in stripe patt of 4 rows M, 2 rows C. Cont until work measures 18(20:23)cm (7:8:9in).

Shape armhole: cast off 4(5:6) sts beg next 2 rows.

Cont until work measures 29(32:36)cm (11½:12½:14¼in), ending with WS row.
*** note patt row.

Shape shoulders and neck: NEXT ROW: k21(22:23), cast off 19(21:23) sts, k21(22:23). On 21(22:23) sts, * dec neck edge on next row. Cast off *. Rejoin yarn to remaining sts at neck edge.
Work * to * again.

LEFT FRONT

Using 3¼mm (US 3) needles and M, cast on 29(31:33) sts. Work 10 rows in moss stitch. Change to 4mm (US 6) needles, stocking stitch and stripe patt as on back. Cont until work measures 18(20:23)cm (7:8:9in) at neck edge.

Shape armhole: (RS facing), cast off 4(5:6) sts beg next row. Cont until work is 12(12:14) rows less than *** noted row on back.

Shape neck: (RS facing), dec neck edge on next 5 rows (20:21:22 sts).
Cont to match back at shoulder. Cast off.

RIGHT FRONT

As for left front to *. Work 1 row. Shape armhole, (WS facing) as left front. Cont as for left front.

SLEEVES

Using 3¼mm (US 3) needles and M, cast on 37(39:41) sts and work 10 rows in moss stitch. Change to 4mm (US 6) needles and stocking stitch. Working in stripe patt as on back, inc each end of 3rd and every foll 4(4:5)th row to 53(57:61) sts. Cont without shaping until work measures 19(22:27)cm (7½: 8½:10½in), placing markers at 18(20:25)cm (7:8:10in). Cast off.

BUTTONBAND

Using 3¼mm (US 3) needles and M, cast on 13(13:15) sts and work in moss stitch until band, when slightly stretched, fits front to neck shaping. Cast off. Sew into place. Mark positions for 8 buttons, the first 2 and last 2 1cm (½in) from bottom and top and 3 sts from each edge; the remaining 4 double spaced evenly between.

BUTTONHOLE BAND

Work to match buttonband making buttonhole positions by: moss 2, yrn, p2tog, moss 5(5:7), p2tog, yrn, moss 2.

COLLAR

Join shoulder seams. With RS facing and using 3¼mm (US 3) needles and M, pick up and knit 67(73:77) sts from neck, starting and finishing halfway across front bands.
Work as follows:
ROWS 1-2: k2, moss to last 2 sts, k2
ROW 3: k2, moss to last 3 sts, inc, k2
Repeat row 3 until work measures 6cm (2½in). Cast off loosely.

Sweater

BACK

As cardigan back to *** noted patt row.

Shape shoulders and neck:
RS facing, k18(19:20) k2tog, turn.
NEXT ROW: p2tog, purl to end. Cast off.
Place 21(23:25) sts on holder. Rejoin yarn to remaining sts, k2tog, knit to end.
NEXT ROW: purl to last 2 sts, p2tog.
Size 1 and 2: change to 3¼mm (US 3) needles and work 4 rows in moss stitch.
Cast off in moss stitch.
Size 3: cast off.

breton cardigan and sweater

SIZES	**1**	**2**	**3**
to fit years	6 mths–1	1–2	2–3
actual chest cm(in)	61(24)	66(26)	71(28)
back length	29(11½)	32(12½)	36(14)
sleeve seam	18(7)	20(8)	25(10)

YARN

Rowan Designer DK wool 50g balls

Cardigan

	1	**2**	**3**
navy (M)	3	3	4
cream (C)	1	1	2

Sweater

	1	**2**	**3**
cream (M)	2	3	3
navy (C)	1	1	2

BUTTONS

8 buttons (cardigan). 3 buttons (sweater sizes 1 and 2).

NEEDLES

1 pair each of 3¼mm (US 3) and 4mm (US 6) needles. Stitch holders (sweater).

FRONT

As back to 12(14:16) rows less than *** noted patt row.

Shape neck: ROW 1: k23(24:25) k2tog turn

ROWS 2–7: dec neck edge, patt. Work 1(3:9) rows.

Sizes 1 and 2: * k6, yrn, k2tog * twice, k2(3)

Change to 3¼mm (US 3) needles and work 3 rows in moss stitch. Cast off in moss stitch.

Size 3: cast off.

Place 11(13:15) sts on holder. Rejoin yarns to remaining sts at neck edge, k2tog, knit to end.

ROWS 2–7: dec neck edge, patt. Work 5(7:9) rows. Cast off.

SLEEVES

As cardigan.

NECKBAND

Join right shoulder seam. With RS facing and using 3¼mm (US 3) needles and M, pick up and knit 12(14:16) sts from side front neck, 11(13:15) sts from holder, 12(14:16) sts from side back neck, 3 sts from side back neck, 21(23:25) sts from holder and 6(6:4) sts from side neck. Work as follows:

Sizes 1 and 2: work 2 rows in moss stitch.

ROW 3: moss 61(69), dec, yrn, moss 2. Work 2 more rows in moss stitch. Cast off.

Size 3: work 5 rows in moss stitch. Cast off loosely.

Making up

CARDIGAN

Join side seams. Join sleeves to markers. Ease sleevehead into armhole, having marker at side seam (see diagram on page 96). Stitch into position. Weave in any loose ends. Sew on buttons.

SWEATER

Sizes 1 and 2: pin shoulder buttonhole band over buttonband. * Join side seams and sleeve seams to markers. Finish as for cardigan *.

Size 3: join shoulder and neckband. Work * to * as sizes 1 and 2: no buttons.

baby sundress and all-in-one

TENSION

23 sts by 32 rows = 10cm (4in) square over stocking stitch using 3¾mm (US 5) needles.

ABBREVIATIONS

See page 96, and

m1 = pick up loop before next st and knit into back of it.

Sundress

BACK

Using 3¼mm (US 3) needles and pink, cast on 83 sts and work as follows:

ROW 1: WS, knit.

ROWS 2–3: ecru, knit.

ROWS 4–5: pink, knit.

Change to 3¾mm (US 5) needles, stocking stitch and stripe pattern of 4 rows ecru, 2 rows pink. Decrease each end of row 15 and every foll 6th row to 59 sts. Cont without shaping until work measures 33cm (13in).

Shape armhole: cast off 2 sts beg next 2 rows. Dec each end of next two rows. Dec each end of next and foll 4 alt rows. Work 3 rows ***. Dec each end of next and foll 4th row. **(37 sts)**

Cont without shaping until work measures 41cm (16in).

Shape neck and shoulders:

NEXT ROW: k13, cast off 11 sts, k13

On 13 sts work as follows:

ROW 1 AND ALT ROWS: WS facing, purl.

ROW 2: dec, knit to last st, inc.

ROW 4: dec, knit to end.

ROWS 5–16: repeat rows 1–4 3 times. **(9 sts)**

ROW 17: dec each end, purl.

ROW 18: dec, knit to end.

ROW 19: as row 17.

Rejoin yarns to remaining sts at neck edge. Work as follows:

ROW 1 AND ALT ROWS: WS facing, purl.

ROW 2: inc, knit to last 2 sts, dec.

ROW 4: knit to last 2 sts, k2tog.

ROWS 5–16: as rows 1–4, 3 times.

ROW 17: dec each end, purl.

ROW 18: knit to last 2 sts, k2tog.

ROW 19: as row 17.

ROW 20: cast off.

FRONT

As back to *** **(41 sts)**

Dec each end of next row.

Shape neck: WS facing, p14 cast off 11 sts, p14.

On 14 sts, work as follows:

ROWS 1–5: dec neck edge.

ROW 6: purl.

ROW 7: dec neck edge, knit.

ROWS 8–9: as rows 6–7.

ROW 10: p3, cast off 1 st, p3.

ROW 11: k3 yrn k1 k2tog.

ROW 12: dec each end, purl.

ROW 13: cast off.

Rejoin yarns to remaining sts at neck edge. Work rows 1–10 as before.

ROW 11: k2tog k1 yrn k3.

ROWS 12–13: as before.

EDGINGS

Front armhole and neck

With RS facing and using 3¼mm (US 3) twinpin and pink, pick up and knit 27 sts from left armhole, 4 sts from shoulder, 11 sts from side neck, 11 sts from centre neck, 11 sts from side neck, 4 sts from shoulder and 27 sts from right armhole. Work as follows:

ROW 1: k26, inc, k3, inc, k32, inc, k3, inc, k27.

ROW 2: ecru, knit.

ROW 3: k27 * m1 k1 m1 k4 m1 k1 m1 * k33, * to * again, k27.

ROW 4: pink, knit.

ROW 5: cast off knitwise.

Back armhole and neck

With RS facing and using 3¼mm (US 3) twinpin and pink, pick up and knit 40 sts from left armhole, 4 sts from shoulder, 18 sts from side neck, 11 sts from centre neck, 18 sts from side neck, 4 sts from shoulder and 40 sts from right armhole. Work as follows:

ROW 1: k39, inc, k3, inc, k46, inc, k3, inc, k40.

ROW 2: ecru, knit.

ROW 3: k40 * m1 k1 m1 k4 m1 k1 m1 * k47, * to * again, k40.

ROW 4: pink, knit.

ROW 5: cast off knitwise.

MAKING UP

Join side seams. Sew on buttons for shoulder fastening. Weave in any loose ends.

baby sundress and all-in-one

All-In-One

BACK

Extension: Using 3¾mm (US 5) needles and ecru, cast on 19 sts. Work in stocking stitch and stripe patt of 4 rows ecru, 2 rows blue throughout.

ROWS 1–8: patt.

ROWS 9–10: cast on 24 sts beg each row. (67 sts)

Cont in patt until work measures 25cm (10in), note patt row *******.

Dec each end of next and every foll 8th row to 59 sts. Cont without shaping until work measures 38cm (15in).

Shape armhole as for sundress.

Cont until work measures 47cm (18½in).

Shape neck and shoulders as for sundress.

FRONT

Left leg: using 3¾mm (US 5) needles and ecru, cast on 24 sts. Stocking stitch 2 rows ecru, 2 rows blue.

Working in stripe patt 4 rows ecru, 2 rows blue, cont as follows ******:

ROW 5: inc, knit to end.

ROW 6: purl to last st, inc.

ROWS 7–8: as rows 5–6, break yarns, leave on spare needle. (28 sts)

Right leg: work as left leg to ******.

ROW 5: knit to last st, inc.

ROW 6: inc, purl to end.

ROWS 7–8: as rows 5–6.

ROW 9: k28 sts of right leg, cast on 11 sts, k28 sts from left leg. (67 sts)

Cont in patt until stripes match on sides at ******* on back. Work shaping as on back and continue to armhole, matching stripes at sides. Work armhole, neck and shoulders as for sundress front.

EDGINGS

Front armhole, neck and back armhole, neck: as for sundress, using blue for pink.

Leg: join side seams. With RS facing and using 3¾mm (US 3) needles and blue, pick up and knit 24 sts from left front leg cast on, 24 sts from back left leg and 6 sts from side of extension. Work as follows: * knit 1 row blue, 2 rows ecru, 1 row blue. Cast off knitwise *. Work other leg to match.

Buttonband (back extension): with RS facing and using 3¾mm (US 3) needles and blue, pick up and knit 3 sts from leg edging, 19 sts from extension cast on and 3 sts from leg edging. Work * to * as leg edging.

Buttonhole band (front centre bottom edge): with RS facing and using 3¾mm (US 3) needles and blue, pick up and knit 3 sts from leg edging, 7 sts from leg, 11 sts from centre front cast on, 7 sts from leg and 3 sts from leg edging. Work as follows:

ROW 1: knit.

ROW 2: ecru, k3 * cast off 1 st, k7 * 3 times, cast off 1 st, k3.

ROW 3: k3 * yrn k7 * 3 times, yrn k3.

ROW 4: blue, knit.

ROW 5: cast off knitwise.

MAKING UP

Weave in any loose ends. Sew on buttons for shoulder and crotch fastenings.

SIZE

to fit	6mths–1
actual chest cm(in)	51(20)

YARN

Rowan Cotton Glacé 50g balls

ecru	3
pink or blue	2

BUTTONS

2 buttons (sundress), 6 buttons (all-in-one).

NEEDLES

1 pair each of 3¾mm (US 3) and 3¾mm (US 5) needles. 3¾mm (US 3) twin pin.

nursery sweaters

TENSION

20 sts by 28 rows = 10cm (4in) square over stocking stitch using 4mm (US 6) needles.

ABBREVIATIONS

See page 96.

BACK

Boy's ABC (navy) version: Using 3¾mm (US 3) needles and red, cast on 59(65:73) sts. Work as follows:

ROW 1: change to M, knit.

ROWS 2–9: *k1 p1* to last st, k1 (moss stitch).

ROW 10: *moss 14(15:16), inc* 3 times, moss to end. (62:68:76 sts)

Girl's 123 (mid-blue) version: Using 4mm (US 6) needles and M, cast on 62(68:76) sts work in stocking stitch as follows:

Both versions: Using 4mm (US 6) needles, work in stocking stitch as follows:

ROWS 1–2: red.

ROWS 3–11: as graph.

ROWS 12–13: green.

ROWS 14–26: as graph.

ROWS 27–28: blue or navy.

ROWS 29–37: as graph rows 3–11.

ROWS 38–39: yellow.

ROWS 40–52: as graph rows 14–26, but read knit rows from left to right and purl rows from right to left to reverse motifs.

ROWS 53–54: orange.

ROWS 55–63: as graph, rows 3–11.

ROWS 64–65: red.

ROWS 66–78: as graph, rows 14–26, size 1 start neck on row 76.

ROWS 79–80: green.

ROWS 81–89: as graph rows 3–11, size 2 start neck on row 82, using M only.

ROWS 90–91: blue or navy.

ROWS 92–94: M, size 3 start neck on row 92.

Shape neck: NEXT ROW: (WS facing) patt 22(23:26) sts, turn.

ROWS 2–3: dec neck edge (following relevant part of graph for patt).

ROWS 4–6: change to 3¾mm (US 3) needles and using M, work in moss stitch.

ROW 7: cast off in moss stitch.

Place centre 18(22:24) sts on holder. Rejoin yarns to remaining sts at neck edge, patt to end. Work 2 more rows from graph, dec at neck edge. Cast off.

FRONT

As back to completion of row 65(71:79).

Shape neck: NEXT ROW: (WS facing), patt 26(28:31) sts, turn. Dec neck edge on next 6(7:7) rows. (20:21:24 sts)

Continue to completion of row 78(84:94). Cast off. Place centre 10(12:14) sts on holder. Rejoin yarns to remaining sts at neck, patt to end. Dec neck edge on next 6(7:7)

rows. Work to completion of row 75(81:91).

NEXT ROW: using M, p4(5:6) p2tog yrn p7 p2tog yrn p5(5:7).

Change to 3¾mm (US 3) needles, work 3 rows in moss stitch. Change to red and purl 1 row. Cast off in red.

SLEEVES

Using 3¾mm (US 3) needles and red, cast on 33(35:37) sts. Change to M and knit 1 row.

ROWS 2–10: moss stitch.

Change to 4mm (US 6) needles and stocking stitch, inc each end of 3rd and every foll 4th row to 53(57:63) sts, working in patt as follows:

ROWS 1–2: red.

ROWS 3–11: follow graph.

ROWS 12–13: green, stocking stitch.

ROW 14: M, purl.

ROWS 15–22: M, moss stitch.

ROWS 23–24: blue or navy, stocking stitch.

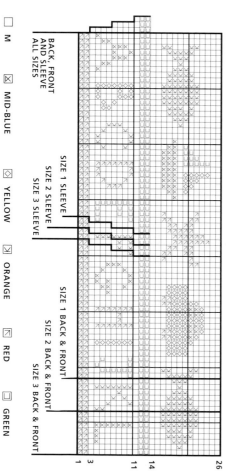

ABC SWEATER FRONT, BACK AND SLEEVE

SIZE 1 SLEEVE
SIZE 2 SLEEVE
SIZE 3 SLEEVE

BACK, FRONT
AND SLEEVE
ALL SIZES

□ M

☒ MID-BLUE

◇ YELLOW

◙ ORANGE

↗ RED

□ GREEN

SIZE 1 BACK & FRONT
SIZE 2 BACK & FRONT
SIZE 3 BACK & FRONT

nursery sweaters

ROW 25: M, knit.

ROWS 26–33: M, moss stitch *.

ROWS 12–33 form sleeve patt, cont as set, to completion of incs and without further shaping until work measures 18(20:25)cm (7:8:10in). Colour stripes in yellow, orange, red, green, blue or navy. Cast off.

NECKBAND

Join left shoulder seam. With RS facing and using 3¼mm (US 3) needles and M, pick up and knit 38(40:46) sts from front neck and 28(32:34) sts from back neck. Work 2 rows in moss stitch.

ROW 3: moss 62(68:76), dec, yrn, moss 2.

ROW 4: moss.

ROW 5: change to red, purl.

ROW 6: cast off loosely.

POINTED EDGING

Girl's 123 version: Using 4mm (US 6) needles and M, cast on 2 sts.

ROW 1: k2.

ROW 2: inc, k1.

ROW 3: k1 p1 inc.

ROW 4: inc, k1 p1 k1.

ROWS 5–8: moss stitch, inc at shaped edge on every row. (9 sts)

ROW 9: moss stitch.

ROWS 10–15: dec at shaped edge on each row, moss stitch. (2 sts)

Repeat rows 1–16 until straight edge fits lower edge of garment, ending after a complete patt repeat.

MAKING UP

Pin right shoulder overlap into place. Measure 12(13:14)cm (4¾:5:5½in) down from shoulder seam, place pin. Set in sleeves between pins and stitch. Join sleeve and side seam. Weave in any loose ends. Sew on buttons. Sew pointed edging to hem of girl's version.

SIZES

	1	2	3
to fit years	6mths–1	1–2	2–3
actual chest cm(in)	59(23)	66(26)	74(29)
back length	29(11½)	32(12½)	36(14)
sleeve seam	18(7)	20(8)	25(10)

YARN

Rowan DK cotton 50g balls

ABC sweater

navy (M)	5	6	7
mid-blue	1	1	1

123 sweater

mid-blue (M)	5	6	7
navy	1	1	1

Both

red	1	1	1
yellow	1	1	1
green	1	1	1
orange	1	1	1

BUTTONS

3 small buttons.

NEEDLES

1 pair each of 3¼mm (US 3) and 4mm (US 6) needles. Stitch holders.

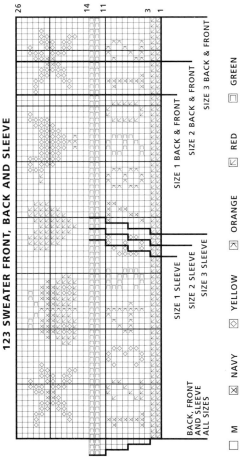

123 SWEATER FRONT, BACK AND SLEEVE

SIZE 1 BACK & FRONT
SIZE 2 BACK & FRONT
SIZE 3 BACK & FRONT

SIZE 1 SLEEVE
SIZE 2 SLEEVE
SIZE 3 SLEEVE

BACK, FRONT AND SLEEVE ALL SIZES

☐ M ☒ NAVY ◇ YELLOW ⊠ ORANGE ☒ RED ☐ GREEN

moss-stitch cardigan and tunic

TENSION

22 sts by 30 rows = 10cm (4in) square over moss stitch using 4mm (US 6) needles.

ABBREVIATIONS

See page 96.

Cardigan

BACK

Using 3¼mm (US 3) needles, cast on 65(73:81) sts and work 10 rows in moss stitch.

Change to 4mm (US 6) needles and cont until work measures 29(32:36)cm (11½:12½:14in).

Shape neck: NEXT ROW: patt 24(27:30) sts, cast off 17(19:21) sts, patt 24(27:30) sts.
* Dec neck edge on next 2 rows. Cast off. *
Rejoin yarn to remaining sts at neck edge and work * to *.

LEFT FRONT

Using 3¼mm (US 3) needles, cast on 32(36:40) sts and work 10 rows in moss stitch.

Change to 4mm (US 6) needles and cont until work measures 25(27:32)cm (10:10½:12½in) ending with a RS row **.

Shape neck: (WS facing) cast off 5(5:6) sts, patt to end. Dec neck edge on next 5(6:6) rows. Cont without shaping until work measures same as back at shoulder. Cast off.

RIGHT FRONT

As for left front to **.

Shape neck: Work 1 row. RS facing, work as for left front.

SLEEVES

Using 3¼mm (US 3) needles cast on 37(39:41) sts and work 10 rows in moss stitch.

Change to 4mm (US 6) needles and inc each end of next and every foll 4(4:5)th row to 53(57:61) sts. Cont without shaping until work measures 18(21:25)cm (7:8¼:10in). Cast off.

BUTTONBAND

Using 3¼mm (US 3) needles, cast on 6 sts and work in moss stitch until band, when slightly stretched, fits front to neck shaping. Cast off. Sew into place. Mark positions for 5 buttons, the first and last 1cm (½in) from top and bottom edges, and remaining 3 evenly spaced between.

BUTTONHOLE BAND

Work to match buttonband, making buttonholes to match button positions by: moss 2, k2tog, yrn, moss 2.

moss-stitch cardigan and tunic

SIZES	1	2	3
to fit years	6mths-1	1-2	2-3
actual chest cm(in)	59(23)	66(26)	74(29)
back length	29(11½)	32(12½)	36(14)
sleeve seam	18(7)	20(8)	25(10)

YARN
Rowan Designer DK wool 50g balls

Cardigan			
green	4	5	6

Tunic			
cream	4	5	6

BUTTONS
5 buttons (cardigan). 1 button (tunic).

NEEDLES
1 pair each of 3¼mm (US 3) and 4mm (US 6) needles.

COLLAR
Join shoulder seams. With RS facing and using 3¼mm (US 3) needles, pick up and knit 67(73:77) sts from neck, beginning and ending halfway across front bands. Work as follows:
ROWS 1–2: k2, moss to last 2 sts, k2.
ROW 3: k2, moss to last 3 sts, inc, k2.
Repeat row 3 until collar measures 6cm (2½in). Cast off loosely in moss stitch.

Tunic

BACK
As for cardigan.

FRONT
As back until work measures 22(23:27)cm (8½:9:10½in).
Divide for neck: patt 32(36:40) sts, cast off 1 st, patt 32(36:40) sts.
On 32(36:40) sts, cont until work measures 25(27:32)cm (10:10½:12½in).
Shape neck:
RS facing, cast off 5(5:6) sts, patt to end. Dec neck edge on next 5(6:6) rows. Cont without shaping until work measures same as back at shoulder. Cast off.
Rejoin yarn to remaining sts at neck edge and work to match.

SLEEVES
As for cardigan.

COLLAR
Join shoulder seams. With RS facing and using 3¼mm (US 3) needles, pick up and knit 67(73:77) sts from around neck. Start and end at front neck edge. Work as for cardigan collar.

Making up

CARDIGAN
✳Measure 12(13:14)cm (4¾:5:5½in) down from shoulder seam, place pin. Set in sleeves between pins and stitch. ✳ Join sleeve and side seams. Weave in any loose ends. Sew on buttons.

TUNIC
Work ✳ to ✳ as for cardigan. Measure 2(3:4)cm (¾:1¼:1½in) up from hem on back and front, place pins. Join side and sleeve seams from pin to cuff. Make small buttonhole loop on righthand side of neck. Sew on button on lefthand side of neck. Weave in any loose ends.

candy-striped sweater and cardigan

TENSION

20 sts by 28 rows = 10cm (4in) square over stocking stitch using 4mm (US 6) needles.

ABBREVIATIONS

See page 96.

Sweater

BACK

Using 3¼mm (US 3) needles and M, cast on 63(67:73) sts and work 10 rows in moss stitch. Change to 4mm (US 6) needles and stocking stitch. Work in stripe pattern as follows:

ROWS 1–7: A.
ROWS 8–11: B.
ROWS 12–13: M.
ROWS 14–20: C.
ROWS 21–23: D.
ROWS 24–28: M.

These 28 rows form stripe pattern repeat.

Cont in patt to completion of row 73(81:91).

Shape neck:

Sizes 1 and 2: NEXT ROW: (WS facing) patt 22(23) sts, turn.

ROWS 2–3: dec neck edge.

ROWS 4–6: change to 3¼mm (US 3) needles and using M, work in moss stitch.

ROW 7: cast off in moss stitch.

Place centre 19(21) sts on holder. Rejoin yarns to remaining sts at neck edge, patt to end. Dec neck edge on next 2 rows. Cast off.

Size 3: NEXT ROW (WS facing), patt 24 sts, turn. * Dec neck edge on next two rows. Cast off *. Place centre 25 sts on holder. Rejoin yarn to remaining sts at neck edge, patt to end. Work * to * again.

FRONT

As back to completion of row 63(71:79).

Shape neck: NEXT ROW: (WS facing), patt 26(28:31) sts, turn. Dec neck edge on next 6(7:9) rows. **(20:21:22 sts)**

Cont to completion of row 76(84:94). Cast off. Place centre 11 sts on holder. Rejoin yarns to remaining sts at neck edge, patt to end. Dec neck edge on next 6(7:9) rows. Work to completion of row 71(79:94).

Size 3: cast off.

Sizes 1 and 2: NEXT ROW: using M p4 p2tog yrn p7 p2tog yrn p5(6).
Change to 3¼mm (US 3) needles, work 4 rows in moss stitch. Cast off.

SLEEVES

Using 3¼mm (US 3) needles and M, cast on 33(35:37) sts and work 10 rows in moss stitch. Change to 4mm (US 6) needles, stocking stitch and stripe patt as on back. Inc each end of 5th and every foll 4th row to 53(57:63) sts. Cont without shaping until work measures 18(20:25)cm (7:8:10in). Cast off.

NECKBAND

Join left shoulder seam. With RS facing and using 3¼mm (US 3) needles and M, pick up and knit 38(40:44) sts from front neck and 28(32:32) sts from back neck.

Sizes 1 and 2: work 2 rows in moss stitch.

ROW 3: moss 62(68), dec, yrn, moss.
ROW 4: moss.
ROW 5: change to C, purl.
ROW 6: cast off loosely.

Size 3: work 4 rows in moss stitch.
ROWS 5–6: as sizes 1 and 2.

Cardigan

BACK

As sweater to completion row 73(81:91).

Shape neck: patt 22(23:24), cast off 19(21:25) sts, patt 22(23:24).

On 22(23:24) sts, * dec neck edge on next two rows. Cast off *.
Rejoin yarn to remaining sts at neck edge and work * to *.

SLEEVES

As sweater.

LEFT FRONT

Using 3¼mm (US 3) needles and M, cast on 31(33:36) sts and work 10 rows in moss stitch. Change to 4mm (US 6) needles, stocking stitch and stripe patt. Cont to completion of row 63(71:79).**

Shape neck: WS facing, cast off 5(6:7) sts beg next row. Dec neck edge on next 6(6:7) rows. **(20:21:22 sts)**

Cont to completion of row 76(84:94).
Cast off.

candy-striped sweater and cardigan

RIGHT FRONT

As for left front to * *. Work 1 row.

Shape neck: RS facing as for left front.

BUTTONBAND

Using 3¼mm (US 3) needles and M, cast on 6 sts and work in moss stitch until band, when slightly stretched, fits front to neck shaping. Cast off. Sew into place. Mark positions for 5 buttons, the first and last 1cm (½in) from top and bottom edges and remaining 3 evenly spaced between.

BUTTONHOLE BAND

Work to match buttonband, making buttonholes to match button positions by: moss 2, k2tog, yrn, moss 2.

COLLAR

Join shoulder seams. Using 3¼mm (US 3) needles and M, with right side facing and beginning and ending at centre of front bands, pick up and knit 67(73:77) sts from neck. Work as follows:

ROWS 1–2: k2, moss to last 2 sts, k2.

ROW 3: k2, moss to last 3 sts, inc, k2.

Repeat row 3 until collar measures 6cm (2½in). Cast off loosely in moss stitch.

Making up

SWEATER

Sizes 1 and 2: pin right shoulder overlap into place. * Measure down 12(13:14)cm (4¾:5:5½in) from shoulder seam, place pin. Set in sleeves between pins and stitch. Join sleeve and side seam. Weave in any loose ends. Sew on buttons.*

Size 3: join right shoulder seam and neckband. Continue from * to * as for sizes 1 and 2; no buttons.

CARDIGAN

Measure down 12(13:14)cm (4¾:5:5½in) from shoulder seam, place pin. Set in sleeves between pins and stitch. Join sleeve and side seams. Weave in any loose ends. Sew on buttons.

SIZES	1	2	3
to fit years	6mths–1	1–2	2–3
actual chest cm(in)	61(24)	66(26)	71(28)
back length	29(11½)	32(12½)	36(14)
sleeve seam	18(7)	20(8)	25(10)

YARN

Rowan DK cotton 50g balls

Sweater

		1	2	3
M	dark pink	2	2	3
A	royal blue	1	2	2
B	light pink	1	1	1
C	dark green	1	2	2
D	yellow	1	1	1

Cardigan

		1	2	3
M	royal blue	2	2	3
A	dark pink	1	2	2
B	light pink	1	1	1
C	lime green	1	2	2
D	yellow	1	1	1

BUTTONS

3 small buttons (sweater size 1 & 2). 5 buttons (cardigan).

NEEDLES

1 pair each of 3¼mm (US 3) and 4mm (US 6) needles. Stitch holders.

little people cardigan

TENSION

20 sts by 28 rows = 10cm (4in) square over stocking stitch using 4mm (US 6) needles.

ABBREVIATIONS

See page 96.

BACK

Using 4mm (US 6) needles and red, cast on 61(65:71) sts. Working in stocking stitch, follow graph.

RIGHT AND LEFT FRONTS

Using 4mm (US 6) needles and red cast on 30(32:35) sts. Working in stocking stitch, follow graph.

SLEEVES

Using 3¼mm (US 3) needles and M, cast on 33(35:37) sts and work 6(8:10) rows in moss stitch. (Every row = * k1 p1 * to last st, k1.) Change to 4mm (US 6) needles and stocking stitch, follow graph.

POINTED EDGING

Work as for sweater, (page 71).

BUTTONBAND

Using 3¼mm (US 3) needles and M, cast on 6 sts and work in moss stitch until band, when slightly stretched, fits front to neck shaping. Break yarn, leave sts on spare needle. Mark positions for 5 buttons, the first 1cm (½in) from bottom edge, the last to be in neck band (two rows above top of buttonband), and remaining 3 evenly spaced between.

68

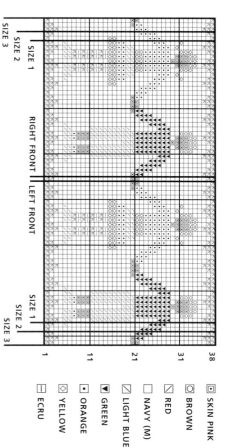

CARDIGAN BACK AND FRONTS

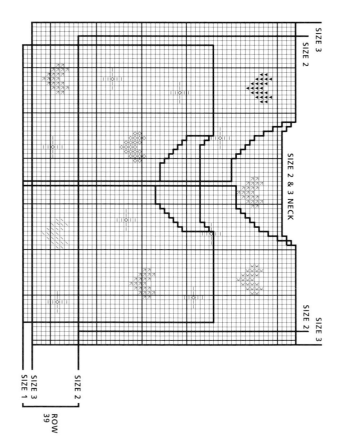

- ⊡ SKIN PINK
- ⊙ BROWN
- ☐ NAVY (M)
- ◪ RED
- ◻ LIGHT BLUE
- ▼ GREEN
- • ORANGE
- ◇ YELLOW
- ☐ ECRU

little people cardigan

BUTTONHOLE BAND

Work to match buttonband, making buttonholes to match button positions by: moss 2, k2tog, yrn, moss 2.
Do not break yarn.

NECKBAND

Join shoulder seams. Using 3¼mm (US 3) needles and M, moss across 6 sts of buttonhole band, with right side facing pick up and knit, 14(18:18) sts from right front neck, 21(27:27) sts from back neck, 14(18:18) sts from left front neck and moss across 6 sts of buttonband. Work as follows:

ROW 1: moss stitch.
ROW 2: moss 2, k2tog, yrn, moss to end.
ROWS 3–5: moss stitch.
ROW 6: cast off in moss stitch.

MAKING UP

Measure 12(13:14)cm (4¾:5:5½in) down from shoulder seam, place pin. Set in sleeves between pins and stitch. Join sleeve and side seams. Weave in any loose ends. Attach front bands. Sew on pointed edging to hem, omitting front bands. Sew on buttons.

SIZES	1	2	3
to fit years	6mths–1	1–2	2–3
chest actual cm(in)	61(24)	66(26)	71(28)
back length	29(11½)	32(12½)	36(14)
sleeve seam	18(7)	20(8)	25(10)

YARN
Rowan DK cotton 50g balls

	1	2	3
☐ navy (M)	4	5	6
⧄ red	1	1	1
⊟ ecru	1	1	1
⬦ yellow	1	1	1
• orange	1	1	1
▶ green	1	1	1
⧄ blue	1	1	1

Small amounts of **skin pink** and **brown**.

BUTTONS
5 buttons.

NEEDLES
1 pair each of 3¼mm (US 3) and 4mm (US 6) needles.

⧄ RED
☐ M
⧄ BLUE
▶ GREEN
• ORANGE
⬦ YELLOW
⊟ ECRU

SLEEVE

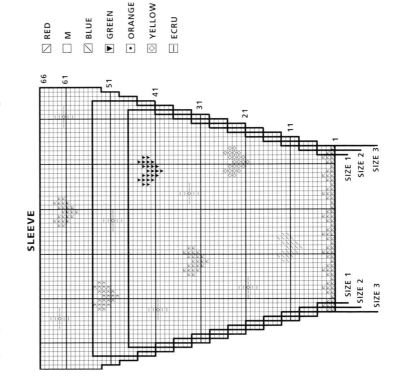

66
61
51
41
31
21
11
1

SIZE 1
SIZE 2
SIZE 3

little people sweater

TENSION

20 sts by 28 rows = 10cm (4in) square over stocking stitch using 4mm (US 6) needles.

ABBREVIATIONS

See page 96.

BACK

Using 4mm (US 6) needles and C, cast on 61(65:71) sts and using stocking stitch, work ROWS 1–3 from little people cardigan back graph (page 68).

Using M, cont to completion of row 75(81:91).

Shape neck:

Sizes 1 and 2: NEXT ROW: (WS facing)
p22(23), turn.

ROWS 2–3: dec neck edge.

ROWS 4–6: change to 3¼mm (US 3) needles, work in moss stitch.

ROW 7: cast off in moss stitch.

Place centre 17(19) sts on holder. Rejoin yarns to remaining sts at neck edge, purl to end. Dec neck edge on next 2 rows. Cast off.

Size 3: NEXT ROW: (WS facing), p23, turn. *
Dec neck edge on next two rows. Cast off. *
Place centre 25 sts on holder. Rejoin yarn to remaining sts at neck edge, purl to end. Work * to * again.

FRONT

As back to completion of row 20(24:30), place motif as follows:

NEXT ROW: knit 17(19:22) M *4 brown, 1M, 4 brown * 9M * to * again, 17(19:22)M. Cont to completion of motif. Using M, work further 12(14:16) rows.

Shape neck:

NEXT ROW: (WS facing), p26(27:28) sts, turn.
Dec neck edge on next 6(6:7) rows. (20:21:21sts)

Continue to completion of row 78(84:94). Cast off. Place centre 9(11:15) sts on holder. Rejoin yarn to remaining sts at neck, purl to end. Dec neck edge on next 6(6:7) rows. Work to completion of row 73(79:94).

Size 3: cast off.

Sizes 1 and 2: NEXT ROW: using M, p4(5)
p2tog yrn p7 p2tog yrn p5.
Change to 3¼mm (US 3) needles, work 3 rows in moss stitch. Change to C and purl 1 row. Cast off in C.

SLEEVES

Using 3¼mm (US 3) needles and C, cast on 33(35:37) sts and work as follows:

ROW 1: change to M, knit. Work 5(7:9) rows in moss stitch.

Change to 4mm (US 6) needles and stocking stitch. Work border graph as for cardigan sleeve (see page 69). Cont cardigan sleeve graph, omitting all motifs.

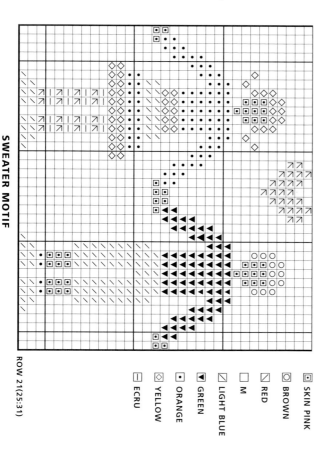

SWEATER MOTIF

ROW 21(25:31)

⊡	SKIN PINK
○	BROWN
⁄	RED
☐	M
•	LIGHT BLUE
▲	GREEN
▪	ORANGE
◇	YELLOW
☐	ECRU

SIZES			
	1	**2**	**3**
to fit years	6mths–1	1–2	2–3
actual chest cm(in)	59(23)	66(26)	71(28)
back length	29(11½)	32(12½)	36(14)
sleeve seam	18(7)	20(8)	25(10)

YARN
Rowan DK cotton 50g balls

☐ navy (M)	5	6	7
☒ red (C)	1	1	1

Small amounts of **yellow, ecru, orange, green, blue, skin pink and brown**

BUTTONS
3 small buttons (size 1 & 2).

NEEDLES
1 pair each of 3¼mm (US 3) and 4mm (US 6) needles.
Stitch holders.

NECKBAND
Join left shoulder seam. With RS facing and using 3¼mm (US 3) needles and M, pick up and knit 35(37:43) sts from front neck and 28(32:32) sts from back neck.

Sizes 1 and 2: work 2 rows moss stitch.

ROW 3: moss to last 4 sts, dec, yrn, moss 2.

ROW 4: moss stitch.

ROW 5: change to C, purl.

ROW 6: cast off loosely in C.

Size 3: work 4 rows in moss stitch.

ROWS 5–6: as sizes 1 and 2.

POINTED EDGING
Using 4mm (US 6) needles and M, cast on 2 sts.

ROW 1: k2.

ROW 2: inc, k1.

ROW 3: k1 p1 inc.

ROW 4: inc, k1 p1 k1.

ROWS 5–8: moss stitch, inc at shaped edge on every row. (9 sts)

ROW 9: moss stitch.

ROWS 10–15: dec at shaped edge on each row, moss stitch. (2 sts)

Repeat rows 1–16 until straight edge fits lower edge of garment, ending after a complete patt repeat.

MAKING UP
Sizes 1 and 2: pin right shoulder overlap into place. ✳ Measure 12(13:14)cm (4¾:5:5½in) down from shoulder seam, place pin. Set in sleeves between pins and stitch. Join sleeve and side seams. Weave in any loose ends. Sew on buttons. Sew pointed edging to hem. ✳

Size 3: join right shoulder seam and neck band. Work ✳ to ✳ as for sizes 1 and 2; no buttons.

aran sweater and cardigan

TENSION

24 sts by 32 rows = 10cm (4in) square over stocking stitch using 3¼mm (US 3) needles.

ABBREVIATIONS

See page 96, and

cn = cable needle.

c4b = place next 2 sts on cn, leave at back of work, k2, k2 from cn.

c4f = place next 2 sts on cn, leave at front of work, k2, k2 from cn.

t3b = place next st on cn, leave at back of work, k2, p1 from cn.

t3f = place next 2 sts on cn, leave at front of work, p1, k2 from cn.

t4b = place next 2 sts on cn, leave at back of work, k2, p2 from cn.

t4f = place next 2 sts on cn, leave at front of work, p2, k2 from cn.

c6b = place next 3 sts on cn, leave at back of work, k3, k3 from cn.

Sweater

BACK

Using 2¾mm (US 2) needles and C, cast on 79(87:95) sts. Change to M and work as follows:

ROW 1: Knit.

ROWS 2–10: * k1 p1 * to last st, k1 (moss stitch).

ROW 11: moss 9(13:17) * inc, moss 5 * 10 times, inc, moss 9(13:17). **(90-98:106 sts)**
Change to 3¼mm (US 3) needles and work as follows:

ROW 1: (WS) moss 5(9:13) [p3 * k4 p4 * twice, k4 p3] * k4 p3 * 3 times, k4 [to] again, moss 5(9:13).

ROW 2: moss 5(9:13) * p4 c4b * twice, p4 k3] * p4 c4b * 3 times, p4 [to] again, moss 5(9:13).

ROW 3: as row 1.

ROW 4: moss 5(9:13) [k3 p3 t3b t3f p2 t3b t3f p3 k3] p3 t3b * t4f t4b * twice, t3f p3, [to] again, moss 5(9:13).

ROW 5: moss 5(9:13) [p3 k3 * p2 k2 * 3 times, p2 k3 p3] k3 p2 k3 p4 k4 p4 k3 p2 k3, [to] again, moss 5(9:13).

ROW 6: moss 5(9:13) [k3 p2 * t3b p2 t3f * twice, p2 k3] p2 t3b p3 c4f p4 c4f p3 t3f p2, [to] again, moss 5(9:13).

ROW 7: moss 5(9:13) [p3 k2 p2 k4 p4 k4 p2 k3] k2 p2 * k4 p4 * twice, k4 p2 k2, [to] again, moss 5(9:13).

ROW 8: moss 5(9:13) [k3 p2 k4 p4 k4 p2 k3] p2 k2 p2 t3b t4f t4b t3f p2 k2 p2, [to] again, moss 5(9:13).

ROW 9: moss 5(9:13) [p3 k2 p2 k4 p4 k4 p2 k2 p3] k2 * p2 k3 * twice, p4 *k3 p2 * twice, k2 [to] again, moss 5(9:13).

ROW 10: moss 5(9:13) [k3 p2 * t3f p2 t3b * twice, p2 k3] p2 * k2 p3 * twice, c4b * p3 k2 * twice, p2 [to] again, moss 5(9:13).

ROW 11: moss 5(9:13) [p3 k3 p2 * twice, p4 * k3 p2 * 3 times, twice, k2 [to] again, moss 5(9:13).

ROW 12: moss 5(9:13) [k3 p3 t3f t3b p2 t3f t3b p3 k3] p2 p3 t3f t3b p2 t3f t3b p3 k2 p2, [to] again, moss 5(9:13).

ROW 13: moss 5(9:13) [p3 * k4 p4 * twice, k4 p3] k2 p2 * k4 p4 * twice, k4 p2 k2, [to] again, moss 5(9:13).

ROW 14: moss 5(9:13) [k3 * p4 c4b * twice, p4 k3] p2 t3f p2 c4f p4 c4f p2 t3b p2, [to] again, moss 5(9:13).

ROW 15: moss 5(9:13) [p3 * k4 p4 * twice, k4 p3] k3 p2 k3 p4 k4 p4 k3 p2 k3, [to] again, moss 5(9:13).

ROW 16: moss 5(9:13) [k3 * p4 k4 * twice, p4 k3] p3 t3f * t4b t4f * twice, t3b p3, [to] again, moss 5(9:13).

Rows 1–16 form patt repeat. Cont in patt until work measures 18(20:23)cm (7:8:9in).

Shape armhole: cast off 5(6:7) sts beg next 2 rows.

Cont until work measures 29(32:36)cm (11½:12½:14in), ending with WS row.

Shape shoulder and neck:

Shoulder

ROW 1: RS facing, patt 30(32:34), turn.

ROW 2: patt.

ROW 3: patt 25(27:29), turn.

ROW 4: patt, ** note patt row.

ROW 5: cast off.

aran sweater and cardigan

SIZES	1	2	3
to fit years	6mths–1	1–2	2–3
actual chest cm(in)	59(23)	66(26)	74(29)
back length	29(11½)	32(12½)	36(14)
sleeve seam	18(7)	20(8)	25(10)

YARN
Rowan Cotton Glacé 50g balls

Sweater			
blue (M)	4	4	5
navy (C)	1	1	1

Cardigan			
dark cream (M)	4	5	5
medium brown (C)	1	1	1

BUTTONS
3 buttons for sweater, 5 buttons for cardigan.

NEEDLES
1 pair each of 2¾mm (US 2) and 3¼mm (US 3) needles, cable needle. Stitch holder for sweater.

Neck and shoulder
ROW 1: RS facing, slip next 25(27:29) sts on holder, patt across remaining sts.
ROWS 2–3: as rows 3–4 of first shoulder. Change to 2¾mm (US 2) needles. Work 4 rows in moss stitch (for buttonband). Cast off in moss stitch.

FRONT
As back to 16(16:18) rows less than noted row ** on back.

Shape neck:
ROW 1: RS facing, patt 34(36:38), turn. Working on these sts:
ROWS 2–7: dec neck edge, patt.
ROW 8: patt.
ROWS 9–12(12:14): dec neck on alt rows, patt. (26:28:29 sts)

Size 3 only: work two more rows.
NEXT ROW: change to 2¾mm (US 2) needles. *k1 p1 * 12(13:14) times, k2tog (k2tog: k1).
ROW 2: [*k1 p1 p1 * 3(3:4) times, yrn, p2tog] twice, *k1 p1 * 4(5:4) times, k1.
ROW 3: moss stitch.
ROW 4: change to C, purl.
ROW 5: cast off.
Place centre 12(14:16) sts on holder. Patt across 34(36:38) sts.
ROWS 2–12: as for first side.
ROW 13: dec neck edge, patt. (25:27:29 sts)
ROWS 14–16(16:18): patt.
Cast off.

SLEEVES
Using 2¾mm (US 2) needles and C, cast on 35(37:39) sts. Change to M and work rows 1–10 as for welt.
ROW 11: moss 7(8:9) * inc, moss 4 * 4 times, inc, moss 7(8:9). (40:42:44 sts)

Change to 3¼mm (US 3) needles and work as follows:
ROW 1: (WS) moss 7(9:11) [p3 * k4 p4 * twice, k4 p3] moss 7(9:11).
ROW 2: moss 7(9:11) [k3 * p4 c4b * twice, p4 k3] moss 7(9:11).
ROW 3: as row 1.
ROW 4: inc, moss 6(8:10) k3 p3 t3b t3f p2 t3b t3f p3 k3 moss 6(8:10), inc.
ROW 5: moss 8(10:12) [p3 k3 * p2 k2 * 3 times, p2 k3 p3] moss 8(10:12).
ROW 6: moss 8(10:12) k3 p2 * t3b p2 t3f * twice, p2 k3 moss 8(10:12).
ROW 7: moss 8(10:12) [p3 k2 p2 k4 p4 k4 p2 k2 p3] moss 8(10:12).
ROW 8: inc, moss 7(9:11) k3 p2 k2 p4 k4 p4 k2 p2 k3 moss 7(9:11), inc.
ROW 9: moss 9(11:13) [as row 7] moss 9(11:13).
ROW 10: moss 9(11:13) k3 p2 * t3f p2 t3b * twice, p2 k3 moss 9(11:13).
ROW 11: moss 9(11:13) [as row 5] moss 9(11:13).
ROW 12: inc, moss 8(10:12) k3 p3 t3f t3b p2 t3f t3b p3 k3 moss 8(10:12), inc.
ROW 13: moss 10(12:14) [as row 1] moss 10(12:14).
ROW 14: moss 10(12:14) [as row 2] moss 10(12:14).
ROW 15: as row 13.
ROW 16: inc, moss 9(11:13) k3 * p4 k4 * twice, p4 k3 moss 9(11:13), inc.
Rows 1–16 form patt repeat. Cont in patt as set and working extra sts in moss stitch to 64(68:72) sts. Cont without shaping until work measures 19(22:27)cm (7½:8½:10½in), placing markers at 18(20:25)cm (7:8:10in). Cast off.

NECKBAND

Join left shoulder seam. With RS facing and using 2¾mm (US 2) needles and M, pick up and knit 16(16:18) sts from front side neck, 12(14:16) sts from holder, 16(16:18) sts from front side neck, 1 st from shoulder seam, 30(32:34) sts from back neck and 4 sts from buttonband. Work as follows:

ROWS 1-2: moss stitch.
ROW 3: moss to last 3 sts, yrn p2tog k1.
ROW 4: moss stitch.
ROW 5: change to C, purl.
ROW 6: cast off.

Cardigan

BACK

As sweater to 29(32:36)cm (11½:12½:14in).
Shape neck and shoulders: patt 30(32:34) sts, cast off 20(22:24) sts, patt 30(32:34) sts.
On 30(32:34) sts:
ROW 1: patt.
ROW 2: cast of 4 sts, patt.
ROW 3: patt ***, note patt row.
ROW 4: cast off.
Rejoin yarn to remaining sts at neck edge.
ROW 1: cast off 4 sts, patt to end.
ROWS 2-3: patt.
ROW 4: cast off.

LEFT FRONT

Using 2¾mm (US 2) needles and C, cast on 39(43:47) sts. Work rows 1-10 as on welt.
ROW 11: moss 7(11:15) * inc moss, 5 * 4 times, inc, moss 7. **(44:48:52 sts)**
Change to 3¾mm (US 3) needles and patt as follows:
ROW 1: (WS) p3 k2 p6 k2 p3 * k4 p4 * twice, k4 p3 moss 5(9:13).
ROW 2: moss 5(9:13) k3 * p4 c4b * twice, p4 k3 p2 k6 p2 k3.
ROW 3: as row 1.
ROW 4: moss 5(9:13) k3 p3 t3b t3f p2 t3b t3f p3 k3 p2 c6b p2 k3.
ROW 5: p3 k2 p6 k2 p3 k3 * p2 k2 * 3 times, p2 k3 p3 moss 5(9:13).
ROW 6: moss 5(9:13) k3 p2 k6 p2 k3.
ROW 7: p3 k2 p6 k2 p3 k2 p4 k4 p2 k2 p3 moss 5(9:13).
ROW 8: moss 5(9:13) k3 p2 k2 p4 k4 p4 k2 p2 k3 p2 k6 p2 k3.
ROW 9: as row 7.
ROW 10: moss 5(9:13) k3 p2 * t3f p2 t3b * twice, p2 k3 p2 k6 p2 k3.
ROW 11: as row 5.
ROW 12: moss 5(9:13) k3 p3 t3f t3b p2 t3f t3b p3 k3 p2 c6b p2 k3.
ROW 13: as row 1.
ROW 14: moss 5(9:13) k3 * p4 c4b * twice, p4 k3 p2 k6 p2 k3.
ROW 15: as row 1.
ROW 16: moss 5(9:13) k3 * p4 k4 * twice, p4 k3 p2 k6 p2 k3.
These 16 rows form patt repeat. Cont in patt until work measures 18(20:23)cm (7:8:9in).
Shape armhole: RS facing, cast off 5(6:7) sts, patt to end. Cont until work is 13(13:15) rows less than *** noted pattern row.

Shape neck: WS facing, cast off 7(8:8) sts, patt to end.
ROWS 2-5: dec neck edge, patt.
ROWS 6-9: dec neck edge on alt rows.
ROW 14: cast off.
Sizes 1 and 2: ROWS 10-13: patt.
Size 3: ROW 10: dec neck edge, patt.
ROWS 11-15: patt.
ROW 16: cast off.

RIGHT FRONT

Cast on and rows 1-10 as Left Front welt.
ROW 11: moss 7 *inc, moss 5 * 4 times, inc, moss 7(11:15). **(44:48:52 sts)**
Change to 3¾mm (US 3) needles and patt as follows:
ROW 1: (WS) moss 5(9:13) p3 * k4 p4 * twice, k4 p3 k2 p6 k2 p3.
ROW 2: k3 p2 k6 p2 k3 * p4 c4b * twice, p4 k3 moss 5(9:13).
ROW 3: as row 1.
ROW 4: k3 p2 c6b p2 k3 p3 t3b t3f p2 t3b t3f p3 moss 5(9:13).
This sets cable positions for Right Front. Cont patts as set until work measures 18(20:23)cm (7:8:9in). Work 1 row.
Shape armhole: WS facing, cast off 5(6:7) sts, patt to end. Cont until work is 12(12:14) rows less than *** noted patt row.
Shape neck: RS facing, cast off 7(8:8) sts, patt to end. Work rows 2-12(12:14) as for Left Front. Cast off.

SLEEVES

As for sweater.

Making up

SWEATER

Join side seams. Join sleeve seams to markers. Place buttonhole band over buttonband and pin together. Set in sleeves (see diagram on page 96) and stitch into position. Weave in any loose ends. Sew on buttons.

CARDIGAN

Join shoulder and side seams. Join sleeve seams to markers. Set in sleeves (see diagram on page 96) and stitch into place. Attach collar: with RS of collar to WS of cardigan ease collar cast-off edge to neck, starting and finishing halfway across front bands. Stitch into position. Weave in any loose ends. Sew on buttons to match buttonholes.

BUTTONBAND

With RS of Left Front facing and using 2¾mm (US 2) needles and M, pick up and knit 71(79:87) sts from front edge. Work 6 rows in moss stitch.

ROW 7: change to C, purl.
ROW 8: cast off.

BUTTONHOLE BAND

Pick up sts on Right Front as on Left Front.
ROWS 1–3: moss stitch.
ROW 4: moss 3 *cast off 1 st, moss 15(17:19) * 4 times, cast off 1 st, moss 3.
ROW 5: moss 3 * yrn, moss 15(17:19) * 4 times, yrn, moss 3.
ROW 6: moss stitch.
ROW 7: change to C, purl.
ROW 8: cast off.

COLLAR

Using 2¾mm (US 2) needles and C, cast on 115(119:125) sts and work as follows:
ROW 1: slip 10 sts onto RH needle. Using M, k95(99:105) turn.
ROW 2: p2tog *k1 p1 * 45(47:50) times, k1 p2tog s1 turn.
ROW 3: s1 k1 psso, moss 91(95:101) k2tog turn.
ROW 4: p2tog, moss 89(93:99) p2tog s1 turn.
ROW 5: s1 k1 psso, moss 89(93:99) k2tog turn.
ROW 6: p2tog, moss 87(91:97) p2tog s1 turn.
ROW 7: s1 k1 psso, moss 87(91:97) k2tog turn.
Cont as set until all C stitches have been used.
NEXT ROW: moss 7(9:7), dec, * moss 8(8:9), dec * 6 times, moss 6(8:6).
Cast off.

bear and tiger hats

TENSION

20 sts by 24 rows = 10cm (4in) square over stocking stitch using 5mm (US 8) needles.

ABBREVIATIONS

See page 96.

BACK

Using 5mm (US 8) needles and C cast on 46 sts and work 20 rows in stocking stitch. Change to M and work as follows:

ROW 1: *k14 k2tog * twice, k14. (44 sts)

ROWS 2–12: stocking stitch.

Start shaping: dec each end of rows 13, 17, 20 and 23 (on tiger hat start contrast on row 21: see graph).

Dec each end of alt rows 25, 27, 29 and 31 (place markers each end of row 29).

Dec each end of every row 32–36. (18 sts)

Cast off.

FRONT

Make as back.

BEAR EARS

Back ears: with RS of back hat facing, and using 5mm (US 8) needles and M, pick up and knit 13 sts between marker and cast off, working as follows:

ROWS 1–6: stocking stitch, starting with a purl row.

ROW 7: dec each end of row.

ROWS 8–9: cast off 2 sts beg each row.

ROW 10: cast off.

Make second ear to match.

Front ears: using front hat and C, work as for back ears.

TIGER EARS

Back ears: pick up 13 sts as for bear ears.

ROWS 1–3: stocking stitch, starting with a purl row.

ROWS 4–9: dec each end of rows.

ROW 10: cast off.

Front ears: using front hat and C, work as for back ears.

MAKING UP

Placing RS together, sew M part of hat and ears. Turn RS out and flat seam C part. Allow C to form a roll hem.

SIZE

To fit   2–3 yrs

YARN

Rowan Magpie 100g hanks

Bear:

beige (M)	1
cream (C)	1

Tiger:

orange (M)	1
black (C)	1

NEEDLES

1 pair 5mm (US 8) needles.

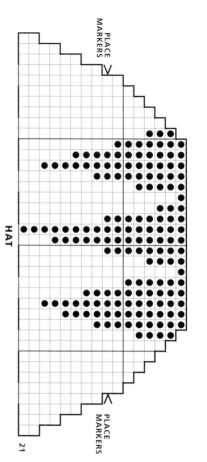

HAT

PLACE MARKERS

PLACE MARKERS

21

☐ M
● C

duffle coats

SIZES

	1	2	3
to fit years	6mths-1	1-2	2-3
actual chest cm(in)	61(24)	68(27)	76(30)
back length	32(12½)	34(13½)	38(15)
sleeve seam	18(7)	21(8½)	26(10½)

YARN

Rowan Magpie 100g hanks   4   4   4

BUTTONS

8 buttons.

NEEDLES

1 pair 4½mm (US 7) needles. Cable needle.

TENSION

18 sts by 32 rows = 10cm (4in) square over moss stitch using 4½mm (US 7) needles.

ABBREVIATIONS

See page 96.

BACK

Using 4½mm (US 7) needles, cast on 55(63:71) sts and work as follows:

ROWS 1– 7: *k1 p1* to last st, k1.

ROW 8: *k1 p1 * 3(4:5) times, k1 [k2 p2 inc p2 k3 * p1 k1 * 3(4:5) times] 3 times. (58:66:74 sts)

ROW 9: *k1 p1 * 3(4:5) times, k1 [p2 k6 p2 * k1 p1 * 3(4:5) times, k1] 3 times.

ROW 10: *k1 p1 * 3(4:5) times, k1 [k2 p6 k3 * p1 k1 * 3(4:5) times] 3 times.

ROWS 11–12: as rows 9–10.

ROW 13: *k1 p1 * 3(4:5) times, k1 [p2 c6b p2 * k1 p1 * 3(4:5) times, k1] 3 times.

ROW 14: as row 10.

ROWS 9–14 form patt repeat. Cont in patt to completion of row 94(100:112).

Cast off.

LEFT FRONT

Using 4½mm (US 7) needles, cast on 37(41:47) sts and work rows 1–7 as for back.

ROW 8: *k1 p1 * 10(11:13) times, k3 p2 inc p2 k3 * p1 k1 * 3(4:5) times.

ROW 9: *k1 p1 * 3(4:5) times, k1 p2 k6 p2 * k1 p1 * 10(11:13) times, k1.

ROW 10: *k1 p1 * 10(11:13) times, k3 p6 k3 * p1 k1 * 3(4:5) times.

ROWS 11–12: as rows 9–10.

ROW 13: *k1 p1 * 3(4:5) times, k1 p2 c6b p2 * k1 p1 * 10(11:13) times, k1.

ROW14: as row 10.

ROWS 9–14 form patt repeat. Cont in patt to completion of row 83(89:99).

** Shape neck: cast off 13(14:16) sts, patt to end.

Dec neck edge on next 6(6:7) rows.
(19:22:25 sts)

Cont to completion row 94(100:112).

Cast off **.

RIGHT FRONT

Using 4½mm (US 7) needles, cast on 37(41:47) sts and work rows 1–4 as for back.

ROW 5: k1 p1 k1, cast off 1 st, patt 11(13:15), cast off 1st, patt to end.

ROW 6: patt 21(23:27), yrn, patt 11(13:15), yrn, patt 3.

ROW 7: as row 1.

ROW 8: *k1 p1 * 3(4:5) times, k3 p2 inc p2 k3 * p1 k1 * 10(11:13) times.

ROW 9: *k1 p1 * 10(11:13) times, k1 p2 k6 p2 * k1 p1 * 3(4:5) times, k1.

This sets position of cable. Cont in patt to completion of row 84(90:100), making further buttonholes on rows 29–30(31–32:35–36), 55–56(59–60:65–66) and 79–80(85–86:95–96).

[1st row: as row 5, 2nd row: patt 22(24:28) sts, yrn, patt 11(13:15) sts, yrn, patt 3 sts]

Work ** to ** as for Left Front.

SLEEVES

Using 4½mm (US 7) needles, cast on 27(27:31) sts and work rows 1–7 as for back.

ROW 8: *k1 p1 * 4(4:5) times, k3 p2 inc p2 k3 * p1 k1 * 4(4:5) times.

ROW 9: *k1 p1 * 4(4:5) times, k1 p2 k6 p2 * k1 p1 * 4(4:5) times, k1.

This sets position of cable. Cont in patt, inc each of next and every foll 5(5:6)th row to 46(50:54) sts, working extra sts in moss stitch. Cont without shaping until work measures 18(21:26)cm (7:8½:10½in). Cast off.

HOOD

Using 4½mm (US 7) needles, cast on 25(27:29) sts. Work as follows:

ROW 1: k1 k1 p1 k1 p2 k6 p2 * k1 p1 * 6(7:8) times.

ROW 2: *p1 k1 * 6(7:8) times, k2 p6 k3 p1 k1.

ROWS 3–4: as rows 1–2.

ROW 5: k1 p1 k1 p2 c6b p2 * k1 p1 * 6(7:8) times.

ROW 6 : as row 2.

Keeping patt correct, inc beg of 10th row and every foll 10th row to 29(31:33) sts. Cont without shaping until work measures 21(25:29)cm (8½:10:11½in) ending with a WS row. RS facing, dec end of next and every foll 10th row to 25(27:29) sts. Work further 9 rows. Cast off.

MAKING UP

Join shoulder seams. Set in sleeve: measure down 12(13:14)cm (4¾:5:5½in) from shoulder seam and place pin. Place sleeve cast-off edge between pins and sew into position. Join side and sleeve seams. Attach hood: fold hood in half and stitch back seam (cable edge is front). With RS together place hood seam to centre back neck, and front edges to beginning of front neck shaping (see photograph), and stitch into position. Weave in any loose ends. Sew on buttons.

78

jester booties

TENSION

24 sts by 32 rows = 10cm (4in) square over stocking stitch using 3¾mm (US 5) needles.

ABBREVIATIONS

See page 96, and

s2 = slip next 2 sts purlwise.

Bootie 1

Sole: using 3¾mm (US 5) needles and A, cast on 41 sts and work as follows:

ROW 1: *inc, k18, inc * twice, k1.

ROWS 2–3: knit.

ROW 4: *inc, k20, inc * twice, k1.

ROWS 5–6: knit.

ROW 7: *inc, k22, inc * twice k1. *(53 sts)*

ROW 8: knit, break A.

ROW 9: using C, knit.

ROW 10: purl.

ROW 11: k1 *yrn, k2tog * to end.

ROW 12: purl.

ROWS 13–14: as rows 9–10.

ROW 15: make hem, fold work at row of holes and knit together 1 stitch from needle and 1 stitch from row 9, across row.

ROW 16: k2tog k51, break C.

Sides:

ROW 17: knit 26A 26B.

ROW 18: using B, k24, inc, k1 yf: using A, inc, k25.

ROW 19: knit 27A 27B.

ROW 20: using B, k25, inc, k1 yf: using A, inc, k26.

ROWS 21–28: inc as set. *(64 sts)*

ROW 29: knit 32A 16B turn.

ROW 30: using B, s1 k13, inc, k1 yf: using A, inc, k15 turn.

ROW 31: s1 k16A k13B turn.

ROW 32: using B, s1 k10, inc, k1 yf: using A, inc, k12 turn.

ROW 33: s1 k13A k10B turn.

ROW 34: s1 k9B yf k10A turn.

ROW 35: s1 k9A k6B turn.

ROW 36: s1 k5B yf k6A turn.

ROW 37: s1 k5A k2B turn.

ROW 38: s1 k1B yf k2A s1 turn. Break yarns.

Shape top of bootie:

ROW 39: using C: k2tog k2 s1 k1 psso turn.

ROW 40: k4 s2 turn.

ROW 41: k3tog k2 s1 k2tog psso turn.

ROW 42: k4 s2 turn.

ROWS 43–52: as rows 41–42 5 times.

ROW 53: k1 k2tog k2 sl k1 psso k1 turn.

ROW 54: k6 s1 turn.

ROW 55: k2tog k4 s1 k1 psso turn.

ROW 56: k6 s1 turn.

ROWS 57–60: as rows 55–56 twice.

ROW 61: k8 turn.

ROW 62: k8 yf s13, break C. *(34 sts)*

Shape ankle cuff:

ROWS 1–4: using B, knit.

ROWS 5–32: *k1 p1 * to end, break B.

ROW 33: using C, purl.

ROW 34: cast off loosely.

Bootie 2

Cast on and work rows 1–16 as Bootie 1.

ROWS 17–38: use B for A and A for B.

ROWS 39 TO END: as Bootie 1.

MAKING UP

Using a flat seam, join sole and back seam. Weave in any loose ends. Attach small bobble (see photo above) obtainable at good craft shops.

SIZE

To fit   6–9 months

YARN

Rowan Designer DK wool: 25g each of 3 colours, A, B and C.

NEEDLES

1 pair 3¾mm (US 5) needles.

79

stripy bag

SIZE

30cm (12in) wide by 32cm (12½in) deep.

YARN

Rowan DK cotton 50g balls

Colourway 1

M	linen	3
A	ecru	1
B	taupe	1
C	mink	1
D	artichoke	1

Colourway 2

M	royal blue	3
A	light pink	1
B	green	1
C	yellow	1
D	dark pink	1

NEEDLES

1 pair 4mm (US 6) needles.

TENSION

20 sts by 28 rows = 10cm (4in) square over stocking stitch using 4mm (US 6) needles.

Cast on 2 sts. Work as follows:

ABBREVIATIONS

See page 96.

FRONT

Using D, cast on 61 sts. Work in stocking stitch and stripe patt as follows:

ROWS 1–7: D.
ROWS 8–11: A.
ROWS 12–13: M.
ROWS 14–20: B.
ROWS 21–23: C.
ROWS 24–28: M.
ROWS 29–56: as rows 1–28.
ROWS 57–79: as rows 1–23.
ROWS 80–96: M. Cast off. Weave in any loose ends.

BACK

Using M, cast on 61 sts and work 84 rows in stocking stitch.
ROW 85: k27 k2tog yrn k3 yrn k2tog k27.
Work 11 more rows. Cast off. Weave in any loose ends.

STRAP

Using D, cast on 5 sts. Work in stocking stitch until strap measures 112cm (44in).
Cast off. Allow edges to curl.

POINTED FRINGE

Use colours randomly but in complete patt repeats (16 rows).
Cast on 2 sts. Work as follows:

ROW 1: k2.
ROW 2: inc, k1.
ROW 3: k1 p1, inc.
ROW 4: inc, k1 p1 k1.
ROWS 5–8: moss stitch, inc at shaped edge on every row. (9 sts)
ROW 9: moss stitch.
ROWS 10–16: moss stitch, dec at shaped edge on every row. (2 sts)
Cont until completion of 6 repeats. Cast off.

MAKING UP

Place RS sides of bag together and sew 3 sides, leaving cast-off edges open. Turn down hem at top to inside and slipstitch it to row 80. Turn bag RS out. Thread strap through top hem. Cross over (half knot) to enable tightening and loosening. Sew one end securely to each bottom corner. Attach fringe.

80

mexican cardigan and sweater

SIZES

	1	2	3
to fit years	6mths–1	1–2	2–3
actual chest cm (in)	61(24)	66(26)	71(28)
back length	29(11½)	32(12½)	36(14)
sleeve seam	18(7)	20(8)	25(10)

YARN

Rowan DK cotton 50g balls

Cardigan			
ecru	2	3	4
dark pink	2	2	3

1 ball each **navy, orange, lime green, emerald green, light blue, yellow**

Sweater			
ecru	2	3	3
dark pink	1	2	2

1 ball each **navy, orange, lime green, emerald green, light blue, yellow**

BUTTONS

5 buttons (cardigan); 3 buttons (sweater size 1 & 2).

NEEDLES

1 pair each of 3¼mm (US 3) and 4mm (US 6) needles.
Stitch holders for sweater.

TENSION

20 sts by 28 rows = 10cm (4in) square over stocking stitch using 4mm (US 6) needles.

ABBREVIATIONS

See page 96.

Cardigan

BACK

Using 4mm (US 6) needles and orange, cast on 62(66:72) sts. Working in stocking stitch, follow graph.

RIGHT AND LEFT FRONTS

Using 4mm (US 6) needles and orange, cast on 31(33:36) sts. Working in stocking stitch, follow graph.

SLEEVES

Using 3¼mm (US 3) needles and pink, cast on 33(35:37) sts and work 8(8:10) rows in moss stitch. (Every row * k1 p1 * to last st, k1.) Change to 4mm (US 6) needles and stocking stitch.

ROWS 1–12: follow graph on page 83. Cont in 12 row patt repeat, inc each end of next and every foll 4th row to 53(57:63) sts, working extra sts into patt. Cont without shaping until work measures 18(20:25)cm (7:8:10in). Cast off.

POINTED EDGING

Using 4mm (US 6) needles and pink, cast on 2 sts.

ROW 1: k2.

ROW 2: inc, k1.

ROW 3: k1 p1 inc.

ROW 4: inc, k1 p1 k1.

ROWS 5–8: moss stitch, inc at shaped edge on every row. (*9 sts*)

ROW 9: moss stitch.

ROWS 10–16: dec at shaped edge on each row, moss stitch. (*2 sts*)

Repeat rows 1–16 until straight edge fits lower edge of garment, ending after a complete patt repeat.

BUTTONBAND

Using 3¼mm (US 3) needles and pink, cast on 6 sts and work in moss stitch until band, when slightly stretched, fits front to neck shaping. Cast off. Sew into place. Mark positions for 5 buttons, the first and last 1cm (½in) from top and bottom edges, and remaining 3 evenly spaced between.

BUTTONHOLE BAND

Work to match buttonband, making buttonholes to match button positions by: moss 2, k2tog, yrn, moss 2.

COLLAR

Join shoulder seams. Using 3¼mm (US 3) needles and pink, with right side facing and beginning and ending at centre of front bands, pick up and knit 67(73:77) sts from neck. Work as follows:

ROWS 1–2: k2, moss to last 2 sts, k2.

ROW 3: k2, moss to last 3 sts, inc, k2.

Repeat row 3 until collar measures 6cm (2½in). Cast off loosely in moss stitch.

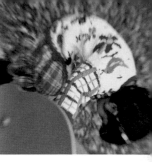

mexican cardigan and sweater

Sweater

BACK

As for cardigan to completion of row 75(85:101).

Shape neck:

Size 1 and 2: NEXT ROW: (WS facing) patt 22, turn.

ROWS 2–3: dec neck edge.

ROWS 4–6: change to 3¼mm (US 3) needles and using M, moss stitch.

ROW 7: cast off in moss stitch.

Place centre 18(22) sts on holder. Rejoin yarns to remaining sts at neck edge, patt to end. Dec at neck edge on next 2 rows. Cast off.

Size 3: NEXT ROW: WS facing, patt 24, turn. * Dec neck edge on next 2 rows. Cast off. * Place centre 24 sts on holder. Rejoin yarns to remaining sts at neck edge, patt to end.
Work * to * again.

FRONT

As back to completion of row 65(75:89).

Shape neck:

NEXT ROW: (WS facing) patt 26(27:29), turn. ** Dec neck edge on next 6(7:7) rows. Work to completion of row 78(88:104). Cast off **. Place centre 10(12:14) sts on holder.

Rejoin yarns to remaining sts at neck edge, patt to end.

Size 3: work ** to **.

Sizes 1 and 2: dec neck edge on next 6(7) rows. Work to completion of row 75(85). **NEXT ROW:** using M, p4 p2tog yrn p7 p2tog yrn p5.

Change to 3¼mm (US 3) needles and work 4 rows in moss stitch. Cast off.

□ M
☒ LIGHT BLUE
⬉ DARK PINK
◇ YELLOW
⬈ ORANGE
⬊ NAVY
◀ LIME GREEN
⊡ EMERALD GREEN

SIZE 3: SWEATER & CARDIGAN, BACK AND FRONTS

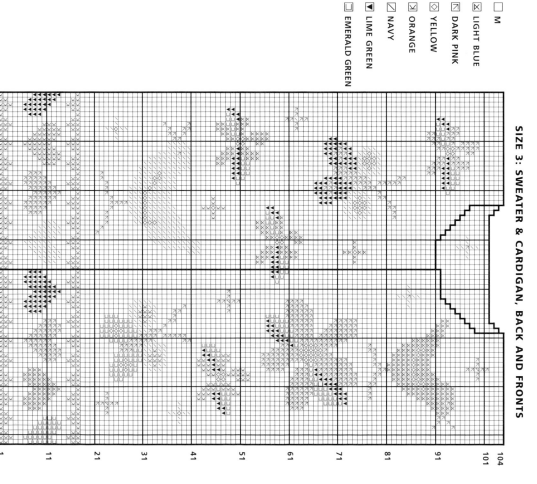

CENTRE FRONT

82

mexican cardigan and sweater

SLEEVES
As for cardigan.

POINTED EDGING
As for cardigan.

NECKBAND
Join left shoulder seam. With RS facing and using 3¼mm (US 3) needles and pink, pick up and knit 38(40:44) sts from front neck and 28(32:32) sts from back neck.

Sizes 1 and 2: work 2 rows in moss stitch.

ROW 3: moss 62(68) dec, yrn, moss 2. Work 2 more rows in moss stitch. Cast off.

Size 3: work 5 rows in moss stitch. Cast off loosely.

Making up

CARDIGAN
Measure 12(13:14)cm (4¾:5:5½in) down from shoulder seam, place pin. Set in sleeves between pins and stitch. Join sleeve and side seams. Weave in any loose ends. Sew pointed edging on to hem, omitting front bands. Sew on buttons.

SWEATER
Size 3: join right shoulder seam and neckband. Set in sleeves as for cardigan. Join sleeve and side seams. Attach pointed edging. Weave in any loose ends.

Sizes 1 and 2: pin right shoulder overlap into place. Continue as for size 3. Sew on buttons.

- ☐ M
- ☒ LIGHT BLUE
- ▨ DARK PINK
- ◇ YELLOW
- ⊠ ORANGE
- ▨ NAVY
- ▶ LIME GREEN
- ☐ EMERALD GREEN

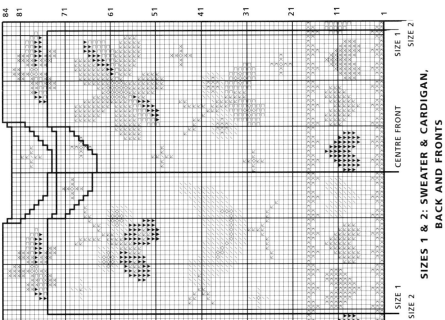

SIZES 1 & 2: SWEATER & CARDIGAN, BACK AND FRONTS

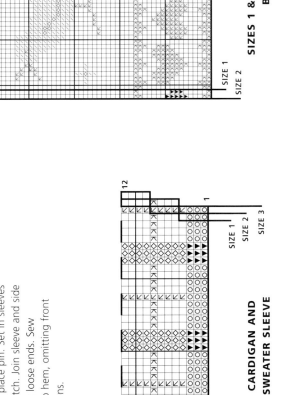

CARDIGAN AND SWEATER SLEEVE

83

fairisle sweater and cardigan

TENSION

20 sts by 28 rows = 10cm (4in) square over stocking stitch using 4mm (US 6) needles.

ABBREVIATIONS

See page 96.

Sweater

BACK

Using 4mm (US 6) needles and M, cast on 61(65:71) sts, working in stocking stitch, follow Fairisle graph (see page 86, 34 row repeat) to completion of row 73(81:91).

Shape neck

Sizes 1 and 2: NEXT ROW: (WS facing) patt 22(23) sts, turn.

ROWS 2-3: dec neck edge.

ROWS 4-6: change to 3¼mm (US 3) needles and using M, work in moss stitch.

ROW 7: cast off in moss stitch.

Place centre 17(19) sts on holder. Rejoin yarns to remaining sts at neck edge, patt to end. Dec neck edge on next 2 rows. Cast off.

Size 3: NEXT ROW: (WS facing), patt 23, turn. * Dec neck edge on next two rows. Cast off *. Place centre 25 sts on holder. Rejoin yarn to remaining sts at neck edge, patt to end. Work * to * again.

FRONT

As back to completion of row 63(71:79).

Shape neck:

NEXT ROW: (WS facing), patt 26(28:30) sts, turn. Dec neck edge on next 6(7:9) rows. (20:21:21 sts)

Cont to completion of row 76(84:94). Cast off. Place centre 9(9:11) sts on holder. Rejoin yarns to remaining sts at neck, patt to end. Dec neck edge on next 6(7:9) rows. Work to completion of 71(79:94).

Size 3: cast off.

Sizes 1 and 2: NEXT ROW: using M, p4 p2tog yrn p7 p2tog yrn p5(6). Change to 3¼mm (US 3) needles, work 3 rows in moss stitch. Change to C and purl 1 row. Cast off in C.

SLEEVES

Using 3¼mm (US 3) needles and C, cast on 33(35:37) sts. Change to M and work as follows:

ROWS 1-6: moss stitch.

Change to 4mm (US 6) needles, stocking stitch and Fairisle, inc each end of 5th and every foll 4th row to 53(57:63) sts working extra stitches into patt. Cont without shaping until work measures 18(20:25)cm (7:8:10in). Cast off.

NECKBAND

Join left shoulder seam. With RS facing and using 3¼mm (US 3) needles and M, pick up and knit 38(40:44) sts from front neck and 28(32:32) sts from back neck.

Sizes 1 and 2: work 2 rows in moss stitch.

ROW 3: moss 62(68), dec, yrn, moss.

ROW 4: moss.

ROW 5: change to C, purl.

ROW 6: cast off loosely.

Size 3: work 4 rows in moss stitch.

ROWS 5-6: as sizes 1 and 2.

LACE EDGING

Using 4mm (US 6) needles and M, cast on 6 sts. Work as follows:

ROW 1: k5, inc.

ROW 2: cast on 2 sts, k1, inc, k2 yf s1 k1 psso k1 yf k2.

ROW 3: k9, inc, k1.

ROW 4: k1, inc, k2 *yf s1 k1 psso k1 * twice, k2.

ROW 5: k11 k2tog.

ROW 6: *s1 k1 psso k4 yf s1 k1 psso * twice, k2.

ROW 7: k8 k2tog.

ROW 8: cast off 3 sts, k3 yf s1 k1 psso k1.

Repeat rows 1-8 until work fits lower edge of sweater, ending with row 8. Cast off.

fairisle sweater and cardigan

SIZES	1	2	3
to fit years	6mths–1	1–2	2–3
actual chest cm(in)	61(24)	66(26)	71(28)
back length	29(11½)	32(12½)	36(14)
sleeve seam	18(7)	20(8)	25(10)

YARN

Rowan DK cotton 50g balls

Sweater

	1	2	3
☐ dark pink (M)	3	3	4
⊘ light pink (C)	1	2	2
⊠ yellow	1	1	1
⊟ ecru	1	1	1

Cardigan

	1	2	3
☐ navy (M)	3	3	4
⊘ light blue (C)	2	2	3
⊠ yellow	1	1	1
⊟ ecru	1	1	1

BUTTONS

3 small buttons (sweater sizes 1 & 2). 5 buttons (cardigan).

NEEDLES

1 pair each of 3¼mm (US 3) and 4mm (US 6) needles. Stitch holders.

Cardigan

BACK

As sweater to completion row 73(81:91).

Shape neck: patt 22(23:24), cast off 17(19:23) sts, patt 22(23:24).

On 22(23:24) sts, * dec neck edge on next two rows. Cast off. *

Rejoin yarn to remaining sts at neck edge and work * to *.

SLEEVES

As sweater.

LEFT FRONT

Using 4mm (US 6) needles and M, cast on 30(32:35) sts. Working in stocking stitch, follow Fairisle graph to completion of row 63(71:79)**.

Shape neck: WS facing, cast off 4(5:6) sts beg next row. Dec neck edge on next 6(6:7) rows. *(20:21:22 sts)*

Cont to completion of row 76(84:94).

Cast off.

RIGHT FRONT

As for left front to **. Work 1 row.

Shape neck: RS facing as for left front.

BUTTONBAND

Using 3¼mm (US 3) needles and M, cast on 6 sts and work in moss stitch until band, when slightly stretched, fits front to neck shaping. Cast off. Sew into place. Mark positions for 5 buttons, the first and last 1cm (½in) from top and bottom edges, and remaining 3 evenly spaced between.

BUTTONHOLE BAND

Work to match buttonband, making buttonholes to match button positions by: moss 2, k2tog, yrn, moss 2.

COLLAR

Join shoulder seams. Using 3¼mm (US 3) needles and M with right side facing, and beginning and ending at centre of front bands, pick up and knit 67(73:77) sts from neck. Work as follows:

ROWS 1–2: k2, moss to last 2 sts, k2.

ROW 3: k2, moss to last 3 sts, inc, k2.

Repeat row 3 until collar measures 6cm (2½in). Cast off loosely in moss stitch.

LACE EDGING

As for sweater. Repeat rows 1–8 until work fits lower edge of cardigan, omitting front bands.

85

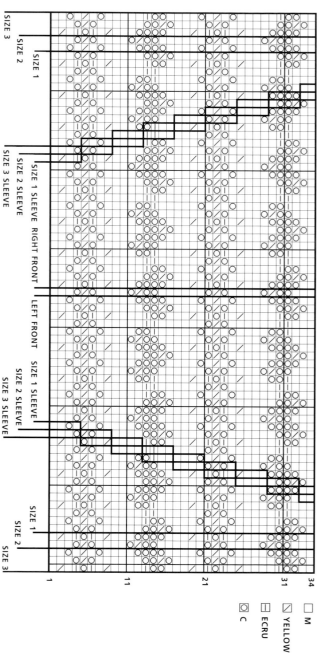

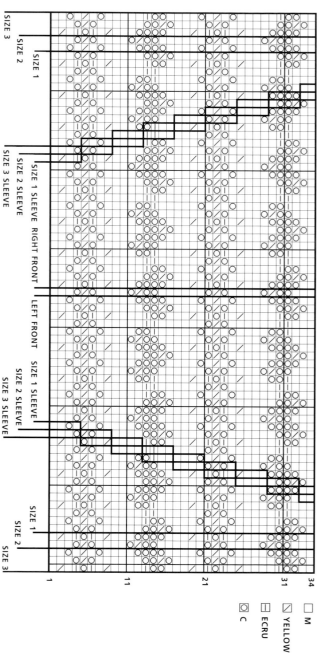

fairisle cardigan

sweater and

Making up

SWEATER

Sizes 1 and 2: pin right shoulder overlap into place. *Measure 12(13:14)cm (4¾:5:5½in) down from shoulder seam, place pin. Set in sleeves between pins and stitch. Join sleeve and side seam. Weave in any loose ends. Sew on buttons. Sew lace edging to hem *.

Size 3: join right shoulder seam and neckband. Continue from * to * as for sizes 1 and 2; no buttons.

CARDIGAN

Measure 12(13:14)cm (4¾:5:5½in) down from shoulder seam, place pin. Set in sleeves between pins and stitch. Join sleeve and side seams. Weave in any loose ends. Join lace edging to hem, omitting front bands. Sew on buttons.

SWEATER & CARDIGAN, FRONTS & BACK AND SLEEVE

SIZE 3
SIZE 2
SIZE 1

SIZE 3 SLEEVE
SIZE 2 SLEEVE
SIZE 1 SLEEVE

RIGHT FRONT

LEFT FRONT

SIZE 1 SLEEVE
SIZE 2 SLEEVE
SIZE 3 SLEEVE

SIZE 1
SIZE 2
SIZE 3

1
11
21
31
34

86

☐ M
◪ YELLOW
◻ ECRU
◉ C

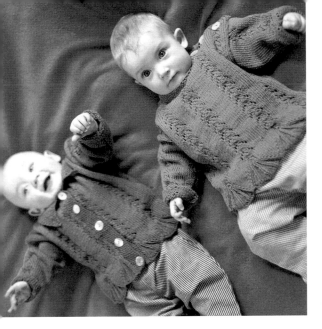

lacy sweater and cardigan

TENSION

24 sts by 32 rows = 10cm (4in) square over stocking stitch using 3¼mm (US 3) needles.

ABBREVIATIONS

See page 96, and

m1 = pick up loop before next st and knit into the back of it.

Sweater

BACK

Using 3¼mm (US 3) needles, cast on 111(117:123) sts and work as follows:

ROW 1: [k2(3:4) * p4 k1 * 4 times] 5 times, k1(2:3).

ROW 2: [p2(3:4) * k4 p1 * 4 times] 5 times, p1(2:3).

ROW 3: [k1(2:3) m1 k1 p2 p2tog * k1 p4 * twice, k1 p2tog p2 k1 m1] 5 times, k1(2:3).

ROW 4: [p3(4:5) k3 * p1 k4 * twice, p1 k3 p2] 5 times, p1(2:3).

ROW 5: [k2(3:4) m1 k1 p3 k1 p2 p2tog k1 p2tog p2 k1 p3 k1 m1 k1] 5 times, k1(2:3).

ROW 6: [p4(5:6) * k3 p1 * 3 times, k3 p3] 5 times, p1(2:3).

ROW 7: [k3(4:5) m1 k1 p1 p2tog * k1 p3 * twice, k1 p2tog p1 m1 k1 k2] 5 times, k1(2:3).

ROW 8: [p5(6:7) k2 * p1 k2 * twice, p1 k2 p4] 5 times, p1(2:3).

ROW 9: [k4(5:6) m1 k1 p2 k1 p1 p2tog k1 p2tog p1 k1 p2 k1 m1 k3] 5 times, k1(2:3).

ROW 10: [p6(7:8) k2 * p1 k2 * 3 times, p5] 5 times, p1(2:3).

ROW 11: [k5(6:7) m1 k1 p2tog * k1 p2 * twice, k1 p2tog k1 m1 k4] 5 times, k1(2:3).

ROW 12: [p7(8:9) k1 * p1 k2 * twice, p1 k1 p6] 5 times, p1(2:3).

ROW 13: [k7(8:9) p1 * k1 p2tog * twice, k1 p1 k6] 5 times, k1(2:3). (101:107:113 sts)

ROW 14: [p7(8:9) * k1 p1 * 3 times, k1 p6] 5 times, p1(2:3).

ROW 15: [k7(8:9) p1 * s1 k1 psso * twice, k1 p1 k6] 5 times, k1(2:3). (91:97:103 sts)

ROW 16: [p7(8:9) k1 p3 k1 p6] 5 times, p1(2:3).

ROW 17: [k7(8:9) p1 s1 k2tog psso p1 k6] 5 times, k1(2:3). (81:87:93 sts)

ROW 18: [p2tog p14(15:16) 4 times, p2tog p13(15:17) p2tog (75:81:87 sts).

Change to lace pattern:

ROW 1: [k4(5:6) yrn k2 s1 k2tog psso k2 yrn k4] 5 times, k0(1:2).

ROW 2: purl.

ROW 3: [k5(6:7) yrn k1 s1 k2tog psso k1 yrn k5] 5 times, k0(1:2).

ROW 4: purl.

ROW 5: [k6(7:8) yrn s1 k2tog psso yrn k6] 5 times, k0(1:2).

ROW 6: purl.

These 6 rows form patt repeat. Cont in patt until work measures 29(32:36)cm (11½:12½:14in), ending with RS row ***.

Shape neck:

Sizes 1 and 2: NEXT ROW: (WS facing) patt 26(28) sts, turn.

ROWS 2–3: dec neck edge.

ROWS 4: change to 2¾mm (US 2) needles and moss stitch.

ROWS 5–6: moss stitch.

ROW 7: cast off in moss stitch.

Place centre 23(25) sts on holder. Rejoin yarns to remaining sts at neck edge, patt to end. Dec neck edge on next 2 rows. Cast off.

87

Size 3: NEXT ROW: (WS facing), patt 30 sts, turn. *Dec neck edge on next two rows. Cast off *. Place centre 27 sts on holder. Rejoin yarn to remaining sts at neck edge, patt to end. Work * to * again.

FRONT

As back until work measures 24(27:31)cm (9½:10½:12in), ending with RS row.

Shape neck:

NEXT ROW: (WS facing), patt 32(34:36) sts, turn. Dec neck edge on next 8 rows. *(24:26:28 sts)*

Cont to match back length at shoulder. Cast off. Place centre 11(13:15) sts on holder. Rejoin yarn to remaining sts at neck, patt to end. Dec neck edge on next 8 rows.

Size 3: work to match first side. Cast off.

Sizes 1 and 2: work to 3 rows less than first side at shoulder.

NEXT ROW: p6 p2tog yrn p8 p2tog yrn p6(8). Change to 2¾mm (US 2) needles, work 4 rows in moss stitch. Cast off in moss stitch.

SLEEVES

Using 2¾mm (US 2) needles, cast on 37(39:41) sts and work 10 rows in moss stitch.

Size 1: inc end row 10.

Size 2: inc each end of row 10.

Size 3: moss 5 (inc, moss 14) twice, inc, moss 5. **(38:41:44 sts)**

Change to 3¾mm (US 3) needles and work as follows:

ROW 1: [k8(9:10) yrn k2 s1 k2tog k2 yrn] twice, k8(9:10).

ROW 2: purl.

ROW 3: k9(10:11) *yrn k1 s1 k2tog k1 yrn* k10(11:12), rep * to *, k9(10:11).

ROW 4: inc, purl to last st, inc.

ROW 5: k11(12:13) *yrn s1 k2tog psso yrn* k12(13:14), rep * to *, k11(12:13).

ROW 6: purl.

These 6 rows place lace as on back. Cont in patt, inc each end of every foll 4th row to 60(63:66) sts working extra stitches in stocking stitch. Cont without shaping until work measures 18(20:25)cm (7:8:10in). Cast off.

NECKBAND

Join left shoulder seam. Using 2¾mm (US 2) needles and M, pick up and knit 14(16:18) sts from side front neck, 11(13:15) sts from holder, 14(16:18) sts from side front neck, 1 st from shoulder seam, 34(36:34) sts from back neck.

Sizes 1 and 2: ROWS 1–2: moss stitch.

ROW 3: moss to last 4 sts, dec, yrn, moss 2.

ROW 4–5: moss stitch.

ROW 6: cast off loosely.

Size 3: work 5 rows in moss stitch. Cast off loosely.

Making up

SWEATER

Sizes 1 and 2: pin right shoulder overlap into place. * Measure 12(13:14)cm (4¾:5:5½in) down from shoulder seam, place pin. Set in sleeves between pins and stitch. Join sleeve and side seams. Weave in any loose ends. Sew on buttons. *

Size 3: join right shoulder seam and neck band. Continue from * to * as for sizes 1 and 2: no buttons.

Cardigan

BACK

As sweater to neck shaping.

Shape neck:

p25(27:29), cast off 25(27:29) sts, p25(27:29).

On 25(27:29) sts, * dec neck edge on next two rows. Cast off. *

Rejoin yarn to remaining sts at neck edge and work * to *.

SLEEVES

As sweater.

LEFT FRONT

Using 3¾mm (US 3) needles, cast on 57(60:63) sts and work as follows:

ROW 1: [k2(3:4) * p4 k1 * 4 times] twice, k2(3:4) * p4 k1 * twice, k1.

ROW 2: p2 k4 p1 k4 [p3(4:5) * k4 p1 * 3 times, k4] twice, k2(3:4).

ROW 3: [k1(2:3) m1 k1 p2 p2tog * k1 p4 * twice, k1 p2tog p2 k1 m1] twice, k1(2:3) m1 k1 p2 p2tog k1 p4 k2.

ROW 4: p2 k4 p1 k3 [p5(6:7) k3 p1 * k4 p1 * twice, k3] twice, p3(4:5).

ROW 5: [k2(3:4) m1 k1 p3 k1 p2 p2tog k1 p3(4:5)] m1 k1 p3 k1 p2 p2tog k2.

ROW 6: p2 k3 p1 k3 [p7(8:9) * k3 p1 * 3 times, k3] twice, p4(5:6).

ROW 7: [k3(4:5) m1 k1 p1 p2tog * k1 p3 * twice, k1 p2tog p1 k1 m1] twice, k1(2:3) m1 k1 p1 p2tog k1 p3 k2.

ROW 8: p2 k3 p1 k2 [p9(10:11) k2 p1 * k3 p1 * twice, k2] twice, p5(6:7).

ROW 9: [k4(5:6) m1 k1 p2 k1 p2tog k1 p2(3:4) m1 k1 p2 k1 m1 k3] twice, k4(5:6) m1 k1 p2 k1 p2tog k2.

lacy sweater and cardigan

ROW 10: p2 k2 p1 k2 [p11(12:13) * k2 p1 * 3 times, k2] twice, p6(7:8).

ROW 11: [k5(6:7) m1 k1 p2tog * k1 p2 * twice, k1 p2tog k1 m1 k4] twice, k5(6:7) m1 k1 p2tog k1 p2 k2.

ROW 12: p2 k2 p1 k1 [p13(14:15) k1 * k1 p1 k2 * twice, p1 k1] twice, p7(8:9).

ROW 13: [k7(8:9) p1 *k1 p2tog * twice, k1 p1 k6] twice, k7(8:9) p1 k1 p2tog k2. *(52:55:58 sts)*

ROW 14: p2 k1 p1 k1 [p13(14:15) *k1 p1 * 3 times, k1] twice, p7(8:9).

ROW 15: [k7(8:9) p1 *s1 k1 psso * twice, k1 p1 k6] twice, k7(8:9) p1 s1 k1 psso k2. *(47:50:53 sts)*

ROW 16: p3 k1 [p13(14:15) k1 p3 k1] twice, p7(8:9).

ROW 17: [k7(8:9) p1 s1 s1 k2tog psso p1 k6] twice, k7(8:9) p1 s1 k1 psso k1. *(42:45:48 sts)*

ROW 18: [p9(9:10) p2tog p5(6:6)] twice, p8(9:10) p2tog. *(39:42:45 sts)*

Change to lace pattern:

ROW 1: [k4(5:6) yrn k2 s1 k2tog psso k2 yrn k4] twice, k4(5:6) yrn k2 s1 k1 psso k1.

ROW 2: purl.

ROW 3: [k5(6:7) yrn k1 s1 k2tog psso k1 yrn k5] twice, k5(6:7) yrn k1 s1 k1 psso k1.

ROW 4: purl.

ROW 5: [k6(7:8) yrn s1 k2tog psso yrn k6] twice, k6(7:8) yrn s1 k1 psso k1.

ROW 6: purl.

These 6 rows form patt repeat. Cont until work measures 24(27:31)cm, (9½:10½:12in), ending with RS row * *.

Shape neck: WS facing, cast off 6(7:7) sts beg next row. Dec neck edge on next 10(10:11) rows. *(23:25:27 sts)*

Cont to same length as back at shoulder. Cast off.

RIGHT FRONT

Using 3¼mm (US 3) needles, cast on 57(60:63) sts and work as follows:

ROW 1: k2 p4 k1 p4 k1 [k2(3:4) * p4 k1 * 4 times] twice, k1(2:3).

ROW 2: p2(3:4) [* k4 k1 * 4 times, p2(3:4)] twice, k4 p1 k4 p2.

ROW 3: k2 p4 k1 p2tog p2 [k1 m1 k1(2:3) m1 k1 p2 p2tog * k1 p4 * twice, k1 p2tog p2] twice, k1 m1 k1(2:3).

ROW 4: p3(4:5) [k3 p1 * k4 p1 * twice, k3 p5(6:7)] twice, k3 p1 k4 p2.

ROW 5: k2 p2tog p2 k1 p3 [k1 m1 k3(4:5) m1 k1 p3 k1 p2 p2tog k1 p2tog p2 k1 p3] twice, k1 m1 k2(3:4).

ROW 6: p4(5:6) [* k3 p1 * 3 times, k3 p7(8:9)] twice, k3 p1 k3 p2.

ROW 7: k2 p3 k1 p2tog p1 [k1 m1 k5(6:7) m1 k1 p1 p2tog * k1 p3 * twice, k1 p2tog p1] twice, k1 m1 k4(5:6).

ROW 8: p5(6:7) [k2 p1 * k3 p1 * twice, k2 p9(10:11)] twice, k2 p1 k3 p2.

ROW 9: k2 p2tog p1 k1 p2 [k1 m1 k7(8:9) m1 k1 p2 k1 p1 p2tog k1 p2tog p1 k1 p2] twice, k1 m1 k4(5:6).

ROW 10: p6(7:8) [* k2 p1 * 3 times, k2 p11(12:13)] twice, k2 p1 k2 p2.

ROW 11: k2 p2 k1 p2tog [k1 m1 k9(10:11) m1 k1 p2tog * k1 p2 * twice, k1 p2tog] twice, k1 m1 k5(6:7).

ROW 12: p7(8:9) [k1 p1 * k2 p1 * twice, k1 p13(14:15)] twice, k1 p1 k2 p2.

ROW 13: k2 p2tog k1 p1[k13(14:15) p1 *k1 p2tog * twice, k1 p1] twice, k7(8:9).

ROW 14: p7(8:9) [* k1 p1 * 3 times, k1 p13(14:15)] twice, k1 p1 k1 p2.

ROW 15: k2 k2tog p1 [k13(14:15) p1 *s1 k1 psso * twice, k1 p1] twice, k7(8:9). *(47:50:53sts)*

ROW 16: p7(8:9) [k1 p3 k1 p13(14:15)] twice, k1 p3.

ROW 17: k1 k2tog p1 [k13(14:15) p1 s1 k2tog psso p1] twice, k7(8:9), **(42:45:48 sts)**

ROW 18: p2tog [p14(15:16) p2tog] twice, p8(9:10). **(39:42:45 sts)**

Change to lace pattern:

ROW 1: k1 k2tog [k2 yrn k8(9:10) yrn k2 s1 k2tog psso] twice, k2 yrn k4(5:6).

ROW 2: purl.

ROW 3: k1 k2tog [k1 yrn k10(11:12) yrn k1 s1 k2tog psso] twice, k1 yrn k5(6:7).

ROW 4: purl.

ROW 5: k1 k2tog [yrn k12(13:14) yrn s1 k2tog psso] twice, yrn k6(7:8).

ROW 6: purl.

These 6 rows form patt repeat. Cont in patt to * on left front. Work 1 row.

Shape neck: RS facing, work as for left front.

BUTTONBAND

Using 2¾mm (US 2) needles, cast on 7 sts and work in moss stitch until band, when slightly stretched, fits front to neck shaping. Cast off. Sew into place. Mark positions for 5 buttons, the first and last 1cm (½in) from top and bottom edges, and remaining 3 evenly spaced between.

BUTTONHOLE BAND

Work to match buttonband, making buttonholes to match button positions by: k1 p1 k1 yrn k2tog p1 k1.

COLLAR

Join shoulder seams. Using 2¾mm (US 2) needles, with right side facing and beginning and ending at centre of front bands, pick up and knit 73(79:85) sts from neck. Work as follows:

ROWS 1–2: k2, moss to last 2 sts, k2.

ROW 3: k2, moss to last 3 sts, inc, k2. Repeat row 3 until collar measures 6cm (2½in). Cast off loosely in moss stitch.

Making up

CARDIGAN

Measure 12(13:14)cm (4¾:5:5½in) down from shoulder seam, place pin. Set in sleeves between pins and stitch. Join sleeve and side seams. Weave in any loose ends. Sew on buttons.

fish sweater

TENSION

20 sts by 28 rows = 10cm (4in) square over stocking stitch using 4mm (US 6) needles.

ABBREVIATIONS

See page 96.

BACK

Using 3¼mm (US 3) needles and red, cast on 66(72) sts and work 10 rows in stocking stitch. Change to M and knit 1 row.

ROWS 2–10: *k3 p3 * to end. Dec **end** of row 10 *(65:71 sts)*.

Change to 4mm (US 6) needles, M and stocking stitch. Work rows 1–18 from graph on page 94.

Work further 4(10) rows in M.

ROW 23(29): Place fish motif k4(7)M, *3 yellow, 3 red * 9 times, 3 yellow, 4(7)M. Cont to completion of motif. *(Row 70:76)*

Change to M and cont to completion of row 81(91).

Shape neck:

NEXT ROW: (WS facing), p21(24), turn. * Dec neck edge on next two rows. Cast off *. Place centre 23 sts on holder. Rejoin yarn to remaining sts at neck edge, purl to end. Work * to * again.

FRONT

As back to completion of row 71(79).

Shape neck:

NEXT ROW: (WS facing), p27(29) sts, turn. Dec neck edge on next 8(7) rows. *(19:22 sts)* Continue to completion of row 84(94). Cast off *. Place centre 11(13) sts on holder. Rejoin yarn to remaining sts at neck, purl to end. Work * to *.

SLEEVES

Using 3¼mm (US 3) needles and red, cast on 36 sts and work 10 rows in stocking stitch. Change to M and knit 1 row.

ROWS 2–10: * k3 p3 * to end. Dec (inc) **end** of row 10. *(35:37 sts)*

Change to 4mm (US 6) needles and stocking stitch, inc each end of 5th and every foll 4th row working in patt as follows:

ROWS 1–18: border graph.

* **ROW 19:** using M, knit.

ROWS 20–26: moss stitch, inc each end rows 21, 26.

ROWS 27–28: using blue, stocking stitch *. Rows 19–28 form sleeve patt repeat. Cont incs as set to 58(64) sts and work stocking stitch colour bands, orange, green, yellow and red until work measures 20(25)cm 8(10)in. Cast off.

SIZES

	2	**3**
to fit years	1–2	2–3
actual chest cm(in)	66(26)	71(28)
back length	32(12½)	36(14)
sleeve seam	20(8)	25(10)

YARN

Rowan DK cotton 50g balls

☐ navy (M)		4	4
☒ red		2	2
⊘ yellow		1	1
⊠ light blue		1	1
▶ green		1	1
⊠ orange		1	1

NEEDLES

1 pair each 3¼mm (US 3) and 4mm (US 6) needles.
Stitch holders.

BACK AND FRONT

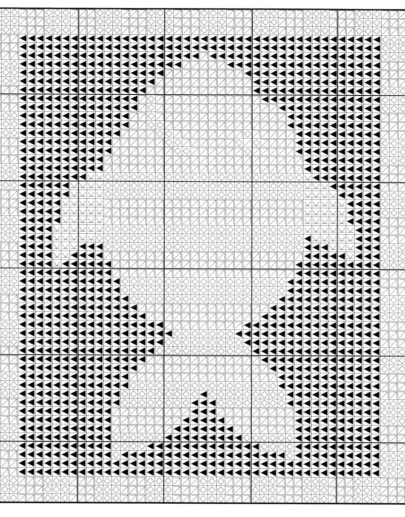

ROW 23(29)

- ◹ RED
- ▼ GREEN
- ⊠ ORANGE
- ◇ YELLOW
- ◺ BLUE

NECKBAND

Join left shoulder seam. With RS facing and using 3¼mm (US 3) needles and M, pick up and knit 14(16) sts from side front neck, 11(13) sts from holder, 14(16) sts from side front neck, 2 sts from side back neck, 23 sts from holder and 2 sts from side back neck. (66:72 sts)

Work as follows:

ROWS 1–5: *k3 p3* to end.

ROWS 6–15: using red, stocking stitch.
Cast off loosely: use 4mm (US 6) needles.

MAKING UP

Join right shoulder seam and neckband. Measure 13(14)cm (5:5½in) down from shoulder seam, place pin. Set in sleeves between pins and stitch. Join sleeve and side seams. Weave in any loose ends.

fish cardigan

SIZES	1	2	3
to fit years	6mths–1	1–2	2–3
chest actual cm(in)	61(24)	66(26)	71(28)
back length	29(11½)	32(12½)	36(14)
sleeve seam	18(7)	20(8)	25(10)

YARN
Rowan DK cotton 50g balls

	1	2	3
☐ navy (M)	5	5	6
☒ red	2	2	2
◇ yellow	1	1	1
◻ blue	1	1	1
▶ green	1	1	1
⊠ orange	1	1	1

BUTTONS
5 buttons.

NEEDLES
1 pair 3¼mm (US 3) and 4mm (US 6) needles.

TENSION
20 sts by 28 rows = 10cm (4in) square over stocking stitch using 4mm (US 6) needles.

ABBREVIATIONS
See page 96, and

m1 = pick up loop before next st and knit into the back of it.

BACK
Using 3¼mm (US 3) needles and M, cast on 61(65:71) sts and knit 10 rows.
Change to 4mm (US 6) needles and stocking stitch. Follow graph.

RIGHT AND LEFT FRONTS
Using 3¼mm (US 3) needles and M, cast on 30(32:35) sts and knit 10 rows.
Change to 4mm (US 6) needles and stocking stitch. Follow graph, placing markers on neck as indicated on graph.

SLEEVES
Using 3¼mm (US 3) needles and M cast on 33(35:37) sts and knit 10 rows.
Change to 4mm (US 6) needles and stocking stitch, follow graph.

FRONT BANDS AND COLLAR
Band: using 3¼mm (US 3) needles and M cast on 6 sts and knit 4 rows.
* ROW 5: k3, cast off 1 st, k2.
ROW 6: k2, yrn, k3.
Knit 20(22:24) rows * Repeat * to * 3 more times. (92:100:108 rows)
Work rows 5–6 again.
NEXT ROW: cast off 3 sts, k3.

Collar:
ROW 1: k3.
ROW 2: k2, turn.
ROW 3: s1, k1.
ROW 4: k2 m1 k1.
ROW 5: k4.
ROW 6: k3, turn.
ROW 7: s1 k2.
ROW 8: k3 m1 k5.
ROW 9: k5.
ROW 10: k4, turn.
ROW 11: s1 k3.
ROW 12: k4 m1 k1.
ROW 13: k6.
ROW 14: k4, turn, s1 k3.
ROW 15: k4 m1 k1, turn, s1 k5.
ROW 16: k6 m1 k1.
ROW 17: k8.
ROW 18: k7, turn.
ROW 19: s1 k6.
ROW 20: k7 m1 k1.
ROW 21: k9.
ROW 22: k8, turn.
ROW 23: s1 k7.
ROW 24: k8 m1 k1.
ROW 25: k10.
ROW 26: k8, turn s1 k7.
ROW 27: k8 m1 k1, turn, s1 k9.
ROW 28: k10 m1 k1.
ROW 29: k12, place marker beg row.

Cont as follows:
* ROW 1: k10, turn.
ROW 2: s1 k9.
ROWS 3–6: k12 *.
Repeat rows 1–6 until shorter edge from collar marker fits from marker on right front neck, round back neck to marker on left front neck. Place marker at shorter edge.
Cont as follows:
ROW 1: k8 k2tog, turn, s1 k8.
ROW 2: k8 k2tog, turn, s1 k8.

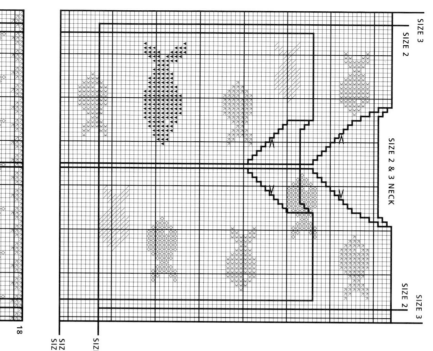

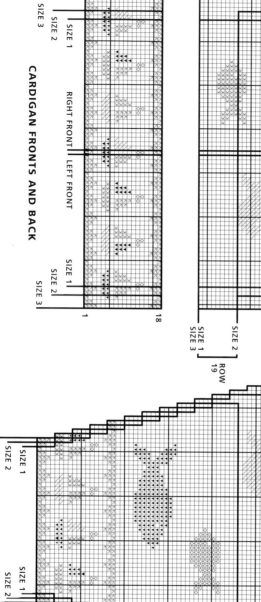

CARDIGAN FRONTS AND BACK

RIGHT FRONT | LEFT FRONT

SIZE 3 / SIZE 2 / SIZE 1

SIZE 2 & 3 NECK

SIZE 2 / SIZE 1 / SIZE 3

CARDIGAN SLEEVE

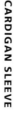

SIZE 3 / SIZE 2 / SIZE 1

ROWS 3–4: k10.

ROW 5: k7 k2tog, turn.

ROW 6: s1 k7.

ROWS 7–8: k9.

ROW 9: k6 k2tog, turn.

ROW 10: s1 k6.

ROWS 11–12: k8.

ROWS 13–14: k4 k2tog, turn, s1 k4.

ROWS 15–16: k6.

ROW 17: k3 k2tog, turn.

ROW 18: s1 k3.

ROWS 19–20: s1 k3.

ROW 21: k2 k2tog, turn.

ROW 22: s1 k2.

ROWS 23–24: k4.

ROW 25: k1 k2tog, turn.

ROW 26: s1 k1.

ROW 27: k3.

ROW 28: k3, cast on 3 sts.

Knit further 94(100:108) rows. Cast off.

MAKING UP

Measure 12(13:14) cm (4¾:5:5½in) down from shoulder seam, place pin. Set in sleeves between pins and stitch. Join sleeve and side seams. Weave in any loose ends. Attach bands and collar, matching markers. Sew on buttons.

M
RED
GREEN
ORANGE
YELLOW
BLUE

STITCH MARKERS

94

flat cats

ABBREVIATIONS
See page 96.

LEGS
Using 3¼mm (US 3) needles and ecru, cast on 24 sts and knit every row. Work as follows:

ROWS 1–8: ecru.
ROWS 9–12: dark green.
ROWS 13–14: light green.
ROWS 15–44: as rows 9–14.
ROWS 45–46: dark green. Break yarn and leave sts on spare needle.

Make second piece, rows 1–46 and cont as follows:

BODY
ROW 47: dark green, knit across second piece then first piece. *(48 sts)*
ROW 48: dark green.
ROWS 49–50: light green.
ROWS 51–66: cont in stripe patt.
ROWS 67–94: red.

HEAD
ROW 95: ecru, ✳ k2tog k2 ✳ to end. *(36 sts)*
ROWS 96–126: ecru.
ROW 127: cast off. Weave in any loose ends.

ARMS (2)
Using 3¼mm (US 3) needles and ecru, cast on 20 sts and knit every row. Work as follows:

ROWS 1–8: ecru.
ROWS 9–32: red.
ROW 33: cast off. Weave in any loose ends.

TAIL
Using 3¼mm (US 3) needles and ecru, cast on 40 sts. Knit 4 rows. Cast off.

MAKING UP
Take a double length of ecru yarn and thread through first row of head (row 95), leave ends loose on RS ✳✳. With RS together fold work in half lengthwise. Join ecru and red sections excluding the top of the head. Refold work, seam to centre and join top of head and inside legs and feet. Turn work RS out. Using filling stuff legs, head and body to give a square shape, not round. Carefully close lower back opening. Fold arms in half lengthways and sew, omitting cast-off edge. Pull double thread ✳✳ together and secure to make neck. Attach arms to body. Roll tail and slipstitch securely. Attach tail to lower back seam.

EARS
Mark 2cm (¾in) in from side edge on head seam and 3cm (1¼in) down on side of head. Using ecru yarn, stitch between markers. Use a length of black wool and a darning needle to embroider the face as shown in the photograph – or make up your own variation. Remember to start and finish at the nose to hide the ends of the yarn.

YARN
Small amounts of Rowan Designer DK wool: we used **ecru**, **dark** and **light green**, and **red**, or **ecru**, **dark** and **light blue**, and **light green**.

FILLING
Washable filling.

NEEDLES
Pair of 3¼mm (US 3) needles. Spare needle.

pattern information

ABBREVIATIONS

The following abbreviations are those most commonly used in all the patterns. Where individual patterns have special abbreviations, these are explained at the beginning of the patterns. Where cast-off stitches are given in the middle of a row, the last stitch of the cast-off is always included in the following instructions.

alt = alternate
beg = beginning
C = contrast colour
cont = continue
dec = decrease by knitting the next 2 stitches together
foll = following
inc = increase by knitting into the front and back of the next stitch
k = knit
k1, p1 rib = (on even number of sts) every row: *k1, p1* to end
= (on odd number of sts) row 1: *k1, p1* to last, k1, row 2: k1 *k1, p1* to end
k2tog = knit next 2 stitches together
k2togb = knit next 2 stitches together through back of loops
k3tog = knit next 3 stitches together
M = main colour
m1 = make stitch by knitting into back of loop before next stitch
moss stitch = (on even number of sts) row 1: *k1, p1* to end, row 2: *p1, k1* to end
= (on odd number of sts) every row: *k1, p1* to last st, k1
p = purl
p2tog = purl next 2 stitches together
p2togb = purl next 2 stitches together through back of loops
p3tog = purl next 3 stitches together
patt = pattern
psso = pass slipped stitch over
rem = remaining

sk = slip next stitch knitwise
sl = slip next stitch
sp = slip next stitch purlwise
stocking stitch = row 1: knit, row 2: purl
st(s) = stitch(es)
tog = together
yb = yarn back
yf = yarn forward
yrn = yarn around needle
** = repeat enclosed instructions number of times indicated by numeral
( ) = brackets refer to larger size(s). Where only one figure is given this refers to all sizes

NEEDLE SIZES

Here is a table showing international sizes.

Metric	British	American
2¾mm	12	2
3mm	11	3
3¼mm	10	3
3¾mm	9	5
4mm	8	6
4½mm	7	7
5mm	6	8

HOW TO DO A TENSION SQUARE

Please check your own tension before you start. Some people find that they need to use a smaller needle when knitting cotton. Cast on at least 30 sts and work at least 40 rows. Measure only the sts given (e.g. 22 sts by 28 rows) to check your tension. Remember that one stitch too many or too few over 10cms (4in) can spoil your work. If you have too many stitches, change to a larger needle, or if you have too few, change to a smaller size, and try again until the tension square is correct. Note: yarns from different manufacturers may not knit to these tensions.

IMPORTANT NOTE ON COLOUR KNITTING

Most of the designs in this book involve different-coloured motifs or shapes worked into the main knitting. In the patterns you are advised to use 'block knitting' or 'intarsia' technique. This means using separate balls of contrast colours, or shorter lengths wound around bobbins, but NOT carrying the main yarn across the back of the section. This is partly to avoid bulky knitting, but mainly to avoid pulling in the work, which reduces the size of the motifs and distorts the knitting, even changing its size. Please work these areas with separate yarns, twisting them at the colour change to avoid holes forming.

CARE INSTRUCTIONS

Steam your knitting lightly by using a warm iron over a damp cloth. Never let the iron come directly in contact with the knitting. Ease the knitting into shape, or block it out with pins until the steam has completely dried off. For washing instructions, see the yarn's ball bands.

GLOSSARY OF TERMS

UK	US
tension	gauge
cast off	bind off
stocking stitch	stockinette stitch

HOW TO FIT SLEEVE

Sleeve must fit in squarely.
Fit **A** to **A**,
B to **B**
C to **C**.

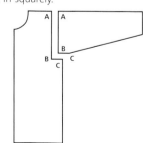